The New London Garden

The New London Garden

GEORGE CARTER

Photography by
MARIANNE MAJERUS

MITCHELL BEAZLEY

Contents

The New London Garden

First published in 2000 by Mitchell Beazley
an imprint of Octopus Publishing Group Ltd,
2–4 Heron Quays, London E14 4JP

Copyright © Octopus Publishing
Group Ltd 2000

Photographs © Marianne Majerus 2000

ISBN 1 84000 347 2

A CIP catalogue copy of this book
is available from the British Library

Executive Editor **Mark Fletcher**
Deputy Art Director and Design **Vivienne Brar**
Project Editor **Michèle Byam**
Contributing Editor **Claire Musters**
Production Controller **Nancy Roberts**
Indexer **Laura Hicks**

Set in Candida

Printed and bound in China by
Toppan Printing Company Limited

ENDPAPERS Grasses in terracotta pots make a
boundary division between an outdoor dining
room and a spectacular Docklands' view of
the Thames.
HALF-TITLE PAGE Peppers growing in a pot on
a Brixton roof terrace.
TITLE PAGE Designer Jonathan Baillie has fixed
1930s stained glass panels to trellis in this
North London garden.
CONTENTS PAGE (left) Mirror-backed Buddha
figures add an exotic air to a Chelsea roof
terrace; (right) A fountain in sculptor Judy
Wiseman's North London garden.

Introduction

In recent years gardening increasingly has been perceived as a 'hip' occupation or hobby. Much of the focus has been concentrated on London, one of the design centres of the world and capital of, arguably, the most famous gardening nation. A wide range of styles and approaches to garden design have emerged in London and this book takes a look behind the scenes to reveal private gardens designed by an eclectic group of people – professional garden designers, garden owners who are creative in quite different fields, and who have employed designers to help fulfil their ideas.

Until recently there was little sign of the quirkiness and fun now found in many London gardens – with notable exceptions, such as the delightful Hampstead garden made in the 1950s by the artist and author Barbara Jones, where

ABOVE A lovely art deco style basket of fruit in stone has been placed under an arbour planted with roses and wisteria to give this Hackney garden the chic appearance of a Parisian garden of the 1920s. This is an example of how to add a strong identity to a garden by simple means.

LEFT A narrow Chelsea plot is given recession by being divided into three distinct areas, linked by a winding, rather than a straight, path. A small rise in the centre helps define the sections, while the simply treated foreground of gravel studded with box balls makes the complex middle ground and distance seem further away.

inventive use was made of bold architectural planting. More often a London garden made between 1950–80 was a scaled down country garden, following formal or informal styles that had hardly changed since Edwardian times. It was rare for anyone to commission a real *coup de théâtre* of the kind described in this book – where the breathtaking effect is all.

The highly influential *The New Small Garden* (Jellicoe and Hurtwood, 1956), which looked at the gardening scene from a modernist viewpoint, included many London gardens. It defined in embryo many of the ideas that have been enthusiastically taken up by garden designers in recent years – including minimalism. The design of urban wild gardens or urban gardens as exterior decoration was not addressed by pre-war modernists, who concentrated on large communal spaces and country gardens. Above all, the book focused on gardens designed by artists, architects, and designers for themselves – underlining the lack at that time of a body of professional garden designers skilled in dealing with the problems of creating interesting city gardens. Certainly the growth in the number and quality of garden designers working in London is one of the key factors in the great creative outburst of the past ten years.

I have divided this book into six thematic chapters, each representative of a particular approach – although, some gardens cross over into more than one area. The chapters represent current design themes, although they all have roots in earlier styles. Some of these are specific to gardening but others come out of architecture, interior decoration, fine art, and even the theatre.

When creating an urban garden there are very different considerations from those of a country garden. Not only is the area available usually smaller, but in cities gardens are more subservient to architecture – the frame of vision being confined to the view from the windows. Such gardens are often seen as outdoor rooms – extensions of relatively confined living spaces. Urban gardeners also have to cope with visual pollution that is beyond their control. Having said this, it is striking how many gardens have been turned into totally private spaces with their own distinct atmosphere.

It was illuminating that many of the garden designers described their creations as theatrical in the sense that the garden provided a 'stage' for the planting to be viewed in an unnatural context. The group within this chapter all make use of an illusionism that relates to the stage designers' art.

As a style, minimalism is usually seen as coming out of modernist architecture, but in gardens it has a much longer pedigree deriving from both Eastern and Western sources. The minimalist gardens in this book have a strong relationship to the buildings with which they are associated and, as such, are very much successful outdoor rooms.

The term exotic generally describes a style of planting that uses hardy or semi-hardy subjects with tropical-looking vegetation. In this section, however, we have also included gardens that conjure up an exotic tropical image without using this type of planting. There are also gardens that use a mix of planting to create a dense tropical feeling in other ways or make the garden seem remote and otherworldly.

It is a paradox that the appearance of naturalism in gardens can only be achieved by highly artificial means.

Decking has a much softer feeling than paving. The house and walls of this Christopher Masson garden in South Kensington have also been clad in a vertical trellis to unify the scheme. Trellising ground floor walls helps to conceal any defects.

ABOVE A North London studio wall has been stained blue/green as a background for a co-ordinated planting of grey and white. Hanging containers designed and made by the artist owners are planted with bluish-white trailing petunias. A nineteenth-century mangle has been painted cobalt blue to form a centrepiece to the composition.

OPPOSITE A miniature Crystal Palace made from what may be have been a nineteenth-century Wardian case (a glass case for plants) contains dolls specially made as portraits of the family. This surreal assemblage is one of the many amusing incidents to be found on a Chelsea roof garden.

Although this chapter shows different approaches to this problem, it concentrates on the way that the aesthetics of plant combinations have been successfully used and reflects the recent awareness of the environmental value of using native plants that provide a habitat for wildlife.

Having the oldest pedigree, formal gardens might be seen as the most traditional group, but nowadays formality has many guises. The underlying theme lies in the geometry of the spatial organization. Formal gardens are particularly suited to London sites, where the careful organization of the space can make the most of a confined area.

The final chapter takes a look at the delightful quirkiness apparent in many London gardens. The sites included have been transformed in a way that defies categorization, although a common theme is to make an environment so beyond the norm that it becomes a virtual fantasy world.

The great variety of garden designs and styles contained in this book graphically illustrate the healthy and inventive state of the art of gardening in London at the start of the new millennium. I feel confident that such wonderful creativity will continue for a long time to come.

Theatrical

Seaside Flotsam and Jetsam

Hampstead

Designer RUTH COLLIER

Gardens can be theatrical in many ways – sometimes in the abstract by utilizing the visual tricks of colour, scale and perspective that are the stock-in-trade of theatre designers, at other times by the clever use of stage properties. It is the latter idea that has been spectacularly employed on this roof terrace. If a theme is carried through with sufficient rigour, as here, the illusion of being somewhere else can work really well. With the most economical means, Tony Morris, the publisher owner of this rather windswept and unappealing flat roof in Hampstead, has conjured up the seaside.

The starting off points for the scheme were the owner's requirements that the garden be of minimum maintenance and reflect his long-term admiration for film maker Derek Jarman's pebble beach garden at Dungeness in Kent.

Seaside planting conforms well to the low-maintenance requirement since it is tough, drought resistant and comes almost virtually colour co-ordinated. Most of the plants in this garden are in the faded grey/green/blue colour range, conjuring up the bleached look of the maritime landscape.

Using fruit crates from Covent Garden market as the containers for growing plants in an earth free zone is a stroke of genius; they are cheap, weigh very little and look like weather worn driftwood. They can also been used as seats and as boxes for grass and pebbles. Ranged around the three sides of the parapet wall they form the *leitmotif* of the whole scheme. Other containers have been added for variety, notably galvanized steel buckets; their shiny silver colour goes very well with the blue grey and black of the various grasses.

The surface of the roof has literally been turned into a beach by covering the paving with a thin layer of sand and pebbles. In the summer, deckchairs supplement the fruit box seating and reinforce the illusion that you are spending a day at the beach. Even the sound of water has been added with a small rock pool.

Anything you might expect to find by the sea is here, arranged into one big oversized still life – anchors, shells,

shrimping nets and fishing net, driftwood, glass floats and artificial seagulls. This sort of themed garden provides endless fun in the opportunity it offers for collecting seaside memorabilia. Although this might sound kitsch, the thoroughness of the conception ensures that it works. The hardware is blended with the planting, which has been largely colour co-ordinated in the bleached neutral shades that are found on sand dunes. It includes sea holly (*Eryngium bourgatii*), santolina, thrift, lavender, *Euphorbia characias*, fennel and *Festuca glauca* – all fashionable plants, but used here because they conjure up the seaside.

This garden is not at all conventional – there are very few flowers, no cut grass and very little green overall. Instead, it focuses on the theatrical, conjuring up an illusion. Many gardeners with such unpromising sites might benefit from the useful self-imposed limitations that such a focused idea brings. Paradoxically, nothing stimulates a gardener's creative energies more than the devising of a single theme, which this particular garden demonstrates so successfully.

ABOVE Sedum, sempervivium and santolina grow out of an amalgam of shells, pebbles and gravel that dress the soil. On the whole, such seaside plants tolerate drying wind, poor soil and general neglect.

PREVIOUS PAGES Even in this incongruous setting, the root terrace is a remarkably realistic evocation of a beach. The roof's surface, which is covered in ordinary gravel, has been diversified with the addition of a few carefully selected pebbles.

RIGHT Tiny details not only reward close inspection but reinforce the maritime theme – such as the tiny glass beads and the seedheads that stud the cascade.

BELOW Heads of sea holly (*Eryngium bourgatii*) are an example of just one of the many seaside plants that populate this garden. These plants make a long term display and add to the blue-grey/purple colour spectrum of the overall scheme.

Architectural Symbolism

Notting Hill

Designers CHARLES JENCKS & MAGGIE KESWICK

The architect Charles Jencks and his late wife, the writer Maggie Keswick, made this wonderfully inventive garden for their redesigned mid nineteenth-century Notting Hill house. Their aim was to create a garden that illustrated their own ideas on the reinvention of a symbolic repertoire for present day architecture. Both felt that Modernism had cleansed the past to such an extent that the richness and creative impetus that can be derived from a cohesive symbolic scheme, as well as a substructure of symbolic decoration and detail, is often distinctly lacking. So they decided to make a garden that, while rich in both meaning and symbolism, was also very much of today. It is in no sense a pastiche of any period, although it has been influenced by the walled garden or Pleasance at Edzell Castle in Scotland, created by Sir David Lindsay in 1604.

Their garden is called the 'Time Garden' and is divided into four quadrants. The main axis has been moved some 3m (10ft) off the centre of the plot in order to line up with the double stairway that gives access into the garden from the *piano nobile* of the house. There is also an entry from the ground floor on this axis.

The two long boundaries of the garden are punctuated by mirrored doorways that are representative of windows on the world. They divide a walk round the garden into twelve sections that symbolize the months of the year. The clockwise route round the garden was devised by Maggie Keswick, who also designed the planting.

The basic structure is defined by a yew hedge, which uses motifs deployed throughout the house – a combination of curves and staggers. The hedge is not clipped flat, but rises to frame the central viewstopper. This diversifies the shape of the central lawn, and not only disguises the fact that it is a standard oblong plot, but also, paradoxically, makes the whole site appear larger. The design also reflects one of Charles Jencks's particular interests – the formulation of appropriate ways to enrich contemporary architecture – thought by many to be too sterile.

Charles Jencks's 'Time Garden' has a central lawn defined by a yew hedge. Around the edge of the garden a brick path takes in a series of incidents; sculpture, inscriptions and planting that are designed both for their symbolism and for beauty.

The idea of dividing areas into four is one that is carried through from the house out into the garden. Here, there can be found the four seasons, the four points of the compass, the four ages of man, the four elements and planting that is representative of four geographical areas. The four prime elements of the garden are: east (spring and China), south (summer and Egypt), west (autumn and America) and north (winter and Europe). Rather than planting each of these areas to solely represent just one season, which would make large parts of the garden boring for three quarters of the year, changing colour schemes have also been devised for the whole garden to represent particular seasons. For instance, in early summer a lively combination of dull purple wisteria in the foreground contrasts with yellow and white plantings further back. In autumn white planting cools the warm yellow foliage of horse chestnut.

As a noted authority and writer on the planting, history and design of Chinese gardens, Maggie Keswick had a particular knowledge of plants from that part of the world. However, her choice for their own garden actually reflects the world's flora, rather than being limited to just one area.

ABOVE The illusionistic viewstopper on the main axis – a mirrored door set into a portico and framed by a false perspective pergola – carries one of the many messages with which the garden is studded. Engraved onto the back of the columns is a text written in reverse so that it can only be read in reflection.

RIGHT The hand rails of the sweeping staircase are luxuriously swathed in purple *Wisteria sinensis*. The colour of this plant is particularly successful alongside the faded blue of the paintwork on the metal staircase.

BELOW Charles Jencks's rebuilding of the house illustrates his views on symbolism in architecture. He has made an entirely new symmetrical façade on the garden front of the early Victorian house. This symmetry is reflected in the garden, although a closer inspection reveals numerous interesting details that are in fact asymmetrically placed.

The planting has been subtly put together to ensure a good, year-round, effect – the herbaceous planting mostly informally arranged in counterpoint to the geometry of the hedges and architecture.

There are innumerable subtleties in the garden. The brick paths change in pattern on each side of the garden to emphasize the change of theme and to add variety to the walkway. No detail is too small to be left to chance and everything has either an overt or hidden message.

Terminating the main axis of the garden is an eye-catcher called the 'Future Pavilion'. Its receding pergola roof and diminishing paired pilasters create a forced perspective that frames a mirrored door. This door appears to open onto the neighbouring garden, although, in fact, it is reflecting the 'Time Garden' itself. The *trompe l'oeil* that is used throughout the house and garden is intended to allude to the idea of seeing into the future.

Only when you get near to the pavilion can you read the inscription 'The Future', which is carved into the centre of the 'door' and looking down to the plinth you read '... is behind you'. Further inscriptions are placed vertically on the back of the pilasters and have been written in reverse so that they can only be read when reflected into the mirror. Seen the right way round they read: E ARRIVA DAL PASSATO TROPPO PRESTO and A LA RECHERCHE DU TEMPS QUI VIENT. *It came from the past too quickly*, and *In search of time to come.*

This garden was also used as a trial run for the truly spectacular garden that Charles Jencks has recently created on the Scottish borders. This is an unusual London garden in that it springs from such an intellectual base, although its careful balance of planting and architecture make it far from sterile. It is a contemporary update of so many ideas from seventeenth- and eighteenth-century gardens that were themselves based on a complex iconography derived from antiquity. It is also rare in London to find such a close and successful correspondence between the interior and exterior design of the house and the garden.

The perimeter walls have a series of 'windows on the world' – mirrors set into window frames. This device works with the mixed planting of ivy and clematis on a trellis to cleverly dissolve the boundaries of the garden.

A Miniature Stage Set

Islington

Designer GEORGE CARTER

Garden photographer Marianne Majerus and her husband Robert Clark, a lecturer in English literature, moved into their Islington house fourteen years ago to find a non-existent garden. The garden area had been built over by a factory workshop so they were literally starting with a blank canvas. This is very unusual and was advantageous in many ways as they had no existing planting to incorporate into the design and no meaningful levels, only the slightly battle-scarred stock London brick walls survived.

The garden is tiny – only 6 x 10m (20 x 30ft). The brief that they gave me was to create a garden that was simple to maintain, interesting throughout the year and made the most of such a confined space. The illusionistic principles of the theatre, which can often be applied to London gardens with great success, were ransacked for ideas to help meet all these requirements.

The prime theatrical device that was employed in this garden was the 'stage flat'. This is a series of receding screens that can add apparent depth to a stage set although here we used the same effect in the garden. The screens were made up of trellis, back planted with evergreens so that the flats or wings became like tall narrow hedges. The screens also widen towards the back of the garden to help the perspectival recession. These have been planted with holly and yew. The walls of the garden are planted largely with evergreen climbers – *Trachelospermum jasminoides* (hardy in London though not in other parts of Britain), *Hydrangea petiolaris* and jasmine. Between each flat a hidden bay of wall space provided many opportunities for contrasting planting that only become visible when someone is actually in the garden.

The central viewstopper, a wall fountain, terminates the vista. It consists of a grey half-urn that drips water into a small pool below. The shellwork of mussels and scallop shells around it was done by the owners, who collected some and bought others from local restaurants – shells can be bought relatively cheaply from specialist shell merchants.

The fountain is made of glass fibre reinforced with a self-coloured, dull grey resin to suggest lead; it is lit up at night for dramatic effect. The scallop and mussel shells were glued to the wall with two part resin glue and a simplified architrave moulding of stained sawn-finish softwood was made to provide a frame for the whole composition.

The ground level of the garden actually raises up away from the house, like a raked stage. This slope has been divided into three shallowly sloping grass steps with a single brick division linking each of the side flats. This gives the illusion of greater depth because it allows the viewer to see more of the grass from ground level than they would if the site were completely level. The grass is always kept very short as this makes the lawn look larger. Running horizontal lines across the garden also helps the space seem wider. Although the garden is longer than it is wide, by using this simple technique, it looks almost square.

The foreground of the garden is made up of a low-retaining wall with, up to the house, a paved terrace that is enhanced by plants in pots. The plants include box topiary and camellia for winter and in summer there is an additional planting of white pelargoniums. This is not a particularly sunny garden but the contrast between the bright grass and the dark evergreens helps to ensure the mixture of light and shade, which is an essential element in all successful gardens. The running water also helps to lighten and animate the garden.

The four-storey house, like many of its period (it was built around 1840), has a first floor drawing room, with a conservatory and balcony leading off it. This means that the garden can also be viewed to great effect from above. Looking down from here, it is almost like being seated in the balcony of a theatre. From this vantage point there is a better view of the pool into which the urn cascades, as well as of the gilded glass ball that appears to float on the surface of the water, adding extra glitter to the garden even on the dullest winter day.

This very small garden is literally like a stage set; it has been provided with a series of stage 'flats' of holly trained on trellis screens. The centrepiece is a theatrical fountain of shells emerging from an urn that drips into a square pool below.

A Shell Grotto Fantasy

Shepherds Bush

Designer BELINDA EADE

LEFT Belinda Eade's assemblages
are in the spirit of seventeenth- and
eighteenth-century grotto work.
She brings together a wide range of
natural materials to create fantastic
images and architectural effects.

BELOW An outbuilding has been
transformed into a magical grotto
by dividing up this small room with
a series of arcaded bays.

Belinda Eade is an artist who specializes in architectural structures made from shells and a variety of found objects and fossils. She has worked all over the world on a number of exotic and bizarre projects and all of these, together with a general interest in garden buildings, make it clear that the taste for follies and for building purely for pleasure has survived unscathed into the twenty-first century.

In creating this garden and shell room for herself she has continued a tradition that can be traced from ancient Rome through Renaissance Italy to seventeenth- and eighteenth-century Britain. However, she has added a contemporary cast to this ancient obsession and updated the genre in order to make it suit her small London garden.

This garden evolved over a long period of time rather than being designed as a coherent, predetermined plan. Having time is a great luxury for designers and often only occurs when they are working on their own gardens. They can experiment at home in a way that is very rarely possible with clients because of the tight time scales involved in creating gardens to commission. Belinda Eade found herself responding to the space available and used whatever materials were to hand. These limitations were actually a help rather than a hindrance to her and it is certainly true that limiting factors can often stimulate ideas.

The prime aim in creating this garden was to construct a place that was both peaceful and mysterious. This was not easy in a space of only 8sq m (25sq ft), but Belinda Eade was able to respond to what she found already there. What had been an inconveniently sited lean-to kitchen at the back of the house was turned, over a period of time, into a grotto. The kitchen was moved inside and this new indoor/outdoor room formed the link between house and garden. It was designed as the main entrance to the garden and its door frames the principal viewstopper – a figurative fountain positioned against the boundary wall of the garden. Not many town gardens have the luxury of being able to 'throw away' a room for this apparently frivolous purpose, but it really does make this garden work. And the space has still retained an important function because it is often used in summer for parties and dinners.

The internal shape of the lean-to has been turned into a cave-like piece of architecture by inserting a column and arched screen at its centre, and by 'losing' the corners in shellwork. Serpentine-shaped shelves at dado height add to the illusion that this is not a conventionally shaped room.

The main outdoor feature, the Diana of Ephesus fountain, was made by Belinda Eade from a variety of materials. The figure was recast from an existing sculpture fragment that she then improved by making it deliberately lumpy, bubbly and uneven – not the sort of thing, she says, that would be acceptable in a garden centre. She then turned this into a fountain using water jets that emit water from the figure's breasts into a basin below. The sculpture is framed by a grotto niche in an irregular ruin mode built more or less flat against the wall. Apparent depth has been added using different colours between the niche's centre and its framing arch.

Although this is primarily an architectural garden, the planting has been designed to form an irregular, mostly evergreen, frame to the various features. The largest tree is a mature eucalyptus, behind which Belinda Eade created a hidden seat. She inherited a large bay tree, a tree paeony and a mass of ivy; the latter is particularly appropriate for the new ambience of the place. To these plants she added box, lavender and hebes – all the new plantings were chosen for their foliage rather than for their flowers. A pergola of cast iron columns has been built on the outer wall of the grotto to be planted with grape vines, making a shaded outdoor dining room.

Belinda Eade did all the construction herself and admits, 'I am always surrounded by sand and cement, and never happier than when able to play with it.' You feel she might almost be a reincarnation of Mrs Delaney, the shell artist and craftswoman who designed and built grottoes, rooms, chandeliers and furniture for a wide circle of friends and patrons in the eighteenth century.

The transformed outhouse's walls have all been completely encrusted by Belinda Eade in varied tufa (lightweight volcanic rock), shells, spars and knapped flints.

A Penthouse Riverscape

Docklands

Designer MICHELE OSBORNE

When Michèle Osborne was first consulted about this roof terrace, which has a spectacular view of the River Thames and Docklands, it was to make it as showy as possible. She was asked to combine Hollywood glitz with Japanese understatement – a very difficult brief. What she has come up with is a wonderfully simple space that does have something of the two without slavishly emulating any style. It is a garden pared down to its bare essentials.

The terrace is about 3.5 x 9m (11½ x 29½ft), situated right on the edge of the river but several stories above it. The essential character of the place is open space with exhilarating vistas; the small area really seems part of the larger landscape and Osborne was keen to retain this.

One big problem in such a position is the wind, and this one factor determined the sort of planting that could survive and still look good, rather than bent and broken. Osborne restricted the planting to phormiums and grasses, both of which have a bold effect, look attractive year round and go with the simple bleached effect of the cedar decking. This is a garden where planting has been used very sparingly and is confined to ten large Cretan pots; of varying sizes but all with a similar banded design, their colour goes perfectly with the rest of the scheme.

The blue-grey Batleigh slate contrasts with the overall sandy palette and was used to form a watery monolithic sculpture at the apex of the terrace, and to make a narrow band between the decking and the handrail. This colour was chosen for its surprising similarity to the colour of the Thames, and it forms a clever visual link between the terrace and the river. There is a definite nautical feel to the whole scheme, from the ocean liner handrail to the specially designed reclining beds that sit so comfortably on the cedar decking. Designed by Bowles and Linares, these are made from powder-coated steel and natural woven fibre. The furniture needs to be heavy in this windy setting so the table has a cast concrete top and shelf.

PREVIOUS PAGES An abstract composition of large blue-grey Batleigh slate monoliths set in a bed of slate chips forms the viewstopper to this Docklands roof terrace.

RIGHT The panoramic landscape is very much a part of the effect of this roof terrace. The 'gardened' area has been kept deliberately low so as not to interfere with the exhilarating open horizon of the view.

BELOW Strong shadows, which are one of the characteristics of this unshaded site, have been exploited, as have the contrasting effects of light and dark, to make compositions of sharply defined forms. The vertical monoliths contrast with the mainly horizontal emphasis of the site.

Phormium are a very tough and effective planting for this sort of exposed position and Osborne has used them to great effect on several similar schemes. She says they never look tattered, they keep their elegant shape and survive drying winds. Not many plants, she says, will put up with these harsh conditions. The varieties used here all have striped variegations, which has an overall lightening effect. Variegated plants are often difficult to place in a garden as they often visually confuse the form of other plants around them, but here they have been singled out as specimens on their own and look magnificent.

One of the cleverest parts of this design is the way the designer has treated what is in effect the prow of the deck – the pointed apex of the terrace that faces a spectacular view of the Docklands' high-rise skyline. This is the real focal point of the view, and Osborne has cunningly mimicked it in a group of monolith-shaped slabs of slate that visually link the distant urban landscape with the deck, and give vertical emphasis to what is essentially a composition of horizontals. These give sufficient interest to the foreground without detracting from the distant view. The largest central slab has been drilled at the top to allow water to cover its face – a simple device that animates the scene, enlivens the face of the slate and makes yet another link between the deck and the water below.

This is a design where the 'Genius of the Place', as the poet Alexander Pope put it, has been consulted and the result is a very special sort of garden, ideally suited to its setting and the particular prevailing conditions.

Illuminated Geometry

Notting Hill

Designers STEPHEN WOODHAMS & CHARLES WORTHINGTON

Charles Worthington, hairdresser to the rich and famous, left the design of his garden until all the rebuilding and redecoration of his house was complete because he wanted to live there and see exactly how the exterior space of the garden could relate to the strikingly minimal all-white interior. By the time he got to the stage of commissioning Stephen Woodhams to help him realize his plans, he had formed a fairly precise idea of what he wanted.

Primarily, he wanted the garden to be a relaxing and liveable outdoor room, and to achieve this he considered aspects of a garden that others might overlook. Light and sound were, for instance, important in achieving the ambience, and to this end bamboo screens were planted (these make a restful rustling sound), which, with the sound of water, to a large extent counteracts the roar of the city. Subtle light effects have also been built into the garden with some of the fittings also designed by Woodhams.

The garden, in total measuring about 10 x 6m (30 x 20ft), is approached via a large deck that is the full width of the house. Three steps down from this lead to the garden proper, which has been designed to focus attention towards a back-lit glass cascade. A sheer 8m (25ft) wall forms the far boundary to the garden, but the introduction of the eye-catching cascade releases the garden from any sense of confinement that such a feature could have imposed.

The planting of the garden is very simple indeed; box, bamboo and ivy are the chief components, enlivened with pots of white hyacinth, white impatiens and other seasonal white flowers. White and green are in fact the only colours used in this garden and the visual function of each plant has been carefully thought out. Bamboo makes the biggest impact – planted in 60cm (24in) wide beds that have been edged with galvanized steel – the canes have now risen to 6m (20ft) tall, almost embowering the garden with an arched canopy of foliage. Spiral box topiary in white tubs define the four corners of the garden and box has also been used as a castellated hedge down the central axis.

Light is used effectively in this
simple garden – not just in the careful
deployment of artificial light, but also
in the use that is made of reflected
daylight. This hits the white gravel,
white walls and the inflatable
furniture to create a sunny effect.

Apart from the decking, the whole ground surface is covered with white marble chippings that are contained by York stone paving or galvanized steel edging. As the garden has been designed very much for night-time entertainment, lighting is hidden throughout to ensure that the right atmosphere can be created for any occasion.

For such a small garden there are numerous seats and these help to reinforce the idea that it is a furnished outdoor room. A decking seat surrounds the cascade's pool and the terrace is furnished with transparent inflatable armchairs and stools found by Charles Worthington in New York; these seem to epitomize the ethereal quality of the whole garden.

Woodhams' refined detailing and expert installation meant that the garden was created quickly, with minimal disruption to the newly decorated house. Maintenance of the garden is carried out by Woodhams' efficient team, who ensure the garden's pristine elegance continues unchanged, apart from seasonal bedding, throughout the year.

ABOVE Small sites benefit from a highly ordered and sharply detailed geometry, which needs to be carried through to every element of the design. Here a seat (right) has been made using galvanized steel planters that match the the metal edgings of the beds.

RIGHT The sheet of water runs over a backlit sheet of etched glass, adding a subtle sparkle and movement to this restful garden. Though everything seems to be static, the sound of water is supplemented by the rustle of bamboo leaves, both elements working together to animate the garden.

Screened from View

Hampstead

Designer RICK MATHER

The celebrated architect, Rick Mather, has produced many large public schemes, often with interesting landscaping that eschews the standard modernist taste for a version of the eighteenth-century landscape park. Instead, his work reinvents the old ideas of hard geometric shape placed against soft, but controlled, informal planting, and the concept of the garden as an outdoor room. His own roof terrace might be on a different scale to most of his projects but it has the same attention to detail and bold simple concept that characterizes his larger work. It has proved a testing ground and an inspiration for many of his larger works. On a grand scale, his new proposals for the opening up of the London South Bank Arts complex are, in effect, creating a vast roof garden that will form a sweeping amphitheatre overlooking the River Thames.

This garden sits at the top of a five-storey Hampstead house and, surprisingly, doesn't break the visual continuity of the streetscape even though it is almost a storey higher than neighbouring houses. This has been achieved by screening its open sides with translucent polycarbonate panels that shelter the planting from the street and winds to create a micro-climate and providing privacy within the garden.

This method of enclosure is the *leitmotif* of the garden. The slightly obscured polycarbonate sheeting is supported on a grid made up of a basic scaffolding system to which it is fixed with brackets. It lets light through but obscures the vision, so that only a vague image of what is on the other side is given. What would have been an impossibly windy site has now become a haven of calm that heats up quickly in even the most meagre sun. The garden has, in effect, become a greenhouse without a roof.

The garden has two terraced levels, the lower one connecting with a large top floor sitting room so that indoor and outdoor living are closely connected. Rick Mather has, as is his usual practice, paid great attention to the circulation space throughout the house, so that a spiral movement upwards culminates by reaching the garden. Even the

The two levels of this enclosed roof terrace give it the quality of a lush, hanging garden. Flanking the steps between the levels are pots of the evergreen *Parahebe lyallii*, which provide masses of white flowers in the early summer.

garden itself has a dynamic element in the way the two levels are visually and practically linked. In the course of conversion the roof structure was reinforced to take the additional weight of soil, which, even though the plants are all grown in containers, is considerable.

The planting has some formal elements to it, such as the four large box cut into bollard shapes placed at the front of the house. Their ghostly outline can be glimpsed from the street, and they provide an architectural repeat pattern that echoes the fenestration of the façades. Most of the planting, however, is free-form; Mediterranean and New Zealand plants predominate and thrive in the sheltered atmosphere. The fact that they flourish here is due to Rick Mather's long experience of the techniques of roof gardening. He likes to tend to the garden himself as, he says, in a hectically busy life it is one of the few things he can still do himself.

This is a rare example of an architect having made a plantsman's garden that is nevertheless design, rather than plant, led. There is something deliciously improbable and gravity defying about any roof garden, but this, more than most, has the air of a lush oasis in the centre of a landscape of unprepossessing city chimneys.

ABOVE Large elongated domes of box make a bold repeat element along the front boundary of the garden. White flowered *Convolvulus cneorum* thrive in the hot micro-climate that has been created by the erection of translucent surrounding walls.

RIGHT Chinese gooseberry
(*Actinidia chinensis*) is trained over
the scaffold pole support structure
of the enclosing screens providing
much-needed shade in summer.

BELOW Actinidia hangs over a
dining table, where its large leaves
and open habit provide a contrast
to the surrounding dense foliage.
Everything is grown in containers,
though this is not apparent from
this overhead shot, where the garden
is seen from the upper level. The
surrounding roofscape can only
be seen from this point.

Decking and Rocks

East Sheen

Designer MATTHEW VINCENT

When Steve and Alison Stonor commissioned Matthew Vincent to design the garden adjoining their 1920s house, they knew they not only wanted it to reflect the simple modern interior but for it to be an extension of of the house, both visually and functionally. As the site had no planting of any value they cleared everything to make a clean canvas for their own plan.

The one element they did keep was the fairly new fence, which is about 2m (6ft) high. This provides a pleasant neutral background to the bold architectural planting they like. They decided to use raised decking for the paths and, instead of conventional beds, would have large tracts of light-coloured pebbles of random sizes that could then be colonized with plants. The simple ground plan makes a bold abstract composition and the decking forms a strong geometrical element, leading the eye to the L-shaped area hidden behind the garage. This visual link makes the most of a small space and suggests a further, hidden, area.

As the design progressed certain ideas emerged. Firstly, it was felt that the pebbles and decking would have a seaside character, and this further influenced some of the detailing – such as the jetty-like projections that support the deck. Vincent introduced grasses to the scheme seeing that their grey, bleached colours make a suitably 'coastal' effect. The shed has been treated as if it were a beach hut, and is stained a faded sea blue. Generally, though, the garden relies on contrasting tones rather than colour. Shadows are important during both day and night. A plain painted wall at the back of the house makes a very effective foil for the graphic foliage of hardy palms, bamboos and phormiums that cast fantastic shadows.

Lighting up the garden at night was given special consideration since that is the time when the owners usually see the garden. The dining room has the best view and its large windows effectively make a fourth wall for the garden at night. Foliage plants are lit from ground level to cast even more dramatic shadows, and each of the decking support

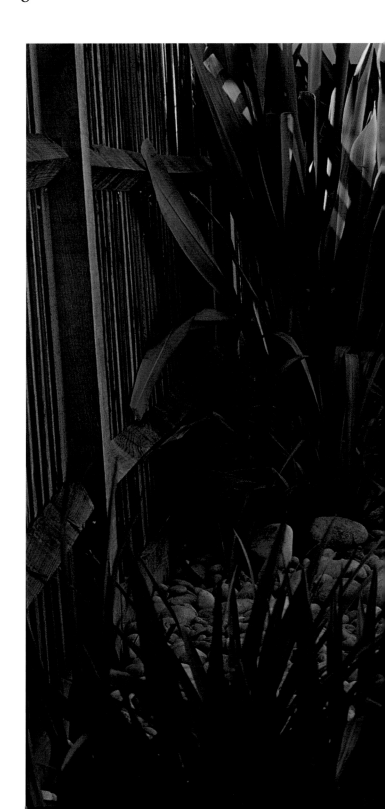

A sunny seaside effect has been achieved in this garden by the simplest of decorative devices. A raised decking walkway makes a comfortable path over large, light-reflecting pebbles, studded with various maritime-style plantings.

posts has a hollow recess in its top for a night light. When they are all lit the walkway becomes a magical bridge.

The decking provides a warm, dry place to sit, but there is also a conventional bench set into a bed retained by railway sleepers against the back boundary fence. The neatest seating area, however, is revealed when a rising portion of the decking is lifted on a sliding central support, out of a specially constructed well, to produce a table. Diners sit with their feet in the well on the non-raised part of the deck. When it is not in use the tabletop is flush with the decking, maximizing the space in this relatively small area.

This garden is very low maintenance. Below the pebbles a weed-suppressant geotextile allows only those subjects planted through it to thrive. The small lawn requires mowing, but otherwise only a little weeding is needed in the raised bed.

There is also a front garden, but this has been treated in a conventional way, to make the discovery of the main garden a wonderful surprise when it is first glimpsed from inside the house. This garden is a perfect example of how to integrate a modern, simple scheme with a type of architecture that you might initially assume needs a more traditional garden.

ABOVE Festucas planted in holes in the geotextile below the pebbles articulate this miniature landscape. Very few plants are needed in such a setting – sparseness usually looks best in this context.

PREVIOUS PAGES At night the garden is made dramatic by ground level spot lights that cast interesting shadows. The support posts for the decking all have recesses for wax night lights, which delineate the path in a rather magical way.

RIGHT A grey-blue stained garden
shed reinforces the bleached seaside
air of the garden, the colour giving
it the air of a beach hut. Grasses
planted in a window box hide the
prosaic contents of the shed that
include bikes and mowers.

BELOW Striped *Phormium* 'Jester' are
lit by long armed low voltage spots,
to give them a striking graphic
quality at night. This means that
after dark their shape, rather than
their colour, is emphasized.

Understated Orientalism

Kensington

Designer JONATHAN BELL

Jonathan Bell's own house and garden in Kensington is something of a test ground for the work he does for clients in England, mainland Europe and North America. His work, which is often done alongside Minimalist architect John Pawson, is reductionist. No unnecessary detail is allowed, and it consequently has a very fresh, spacious feel.

For a garden that appears so confidently perfect it is surprising to find that, here in his own space, Jonathan Bell experiments constantly, and its present state is a refinement of earlier incarnations tinkered with over a long period.

The garden area he and his wife originally had was only about 6 x 9m (20 x 30ft). Out of this he took 5 x 2.5m (15 x 8ft) to build an elegant kitchen/dining room, which he designed himself with an etched glass roof and a clear glass wall overlooking the remaining garden, which is about 4 x 9m (12 x 30ft), with a small 5 x 2.5m (15 x 8ft) patch at the end of the extension. Jonathan Bell is particularly interested in the relationship of indoors and outdoors and many of his schemes, as here, move seamlessly between the two. The garden view actually forms the fourth wall of the room.

The garden had, in the past, been used as the dumping ground for builder's rubble for several adjacent houses, so the first problem was to reduce the ground level to something nearer its original state. This meant the removal of tons of rubbish. The garden is now set on two levels with a dividing wall of rendered concrete that incorporates an outdoor fire bed or hearth, making it comfortable even during winter. The main ground surface is made up of Scottish beach cobbles set with a composition of random York stone flags flush against the surface of the pebbles. These cleverly diversify the surface. The overall effect is rather Japanese in its extreme simplicity; there is no grass and no bare earth in the garden. Because of the compressed soil there is never a problem of weeds in the pebbles and Jonathan Bell says he spends about two hours a year gardening.

Planting is limited to four subjects – *Prunus laurocerasus*, mimosa (*Acacia dealbata*), *Amelanchier lamarckii*, and

Hedera helix – planted against the trellis boundary fencing. A moss garden was originally created but did not survive the ravages of blackbirds, so after much repair and replacement it was finally abandoned. The laurel has been clipped up to make clear stems that form an interesting graphic pattern against the trellis with a wide spreading canopy of leaves.

This is a shady garden that only gets a few hours of sunshine at midday in the height of the summer but, as photographs of the garden show, there is a clarity and cleanness of line that defies the weather and seasons. Such a simplified design does not have the dramatic changes that the seasons bring to most gardens, but there are distinct changes of light, short periods of plant flowering and changes of surface colours when it rains. These subtleties are very telling in such a minimal setting, highlighting elements of nature that are easy to miss in a town setting.

The garden is deliberately not lit by artificial light – it is surrounded by brightly lit buildings and receives plenty of spilt light from the dining room itself. However Jonathan Bell does have plans for a single pink neon tube at ground level in emulation of the minimalist American sculptor Donald Judd. There is also the rather elemental effect of firelight and candlelight when the garden is used at night.

It is a cliche that minimalism equals expensive; in this garden everything has been done with economy in mind. The trellis came straight from a garden centre and was cunningly fixed together without posts showing, using metal 'T' brackets. The furnishings are homemade, and all the materials are readily available.

The garden has also proved to be highly practical as a family space – the Bells' two children enjoy its openness and its swinging seat. The dining room, when its tall (2.5m/8ft) double doors are open, is truly part of the garden, making it unnecessary to have a separate dining terrace.

It is truly a wonderful paradox that this space, which could be called the most 'unnatural' of gardens, has a closer relationship to nature in its broadest sense than many more so-called 'natural' gardens.

An abstract composition is made from broken fragments of York stone paving set nearly flush with the gravel. These, along with the trellis and simple chunky bench, fit in well with the neutral colour scheme.

Exotic

An Exotic Woodland

Stockwell

Designer JASON PAYNE

When palm expert Martin Gibbons moved into his four storey early Victorian Stockwell house about fifteen years ago he was confronted by the sort of garden he hates – an ordered, colour-coded garden that lurched from white to blue to red as the seasons progressed. He removed it all and replaced it with a collection of palms that had previously lived in the conservatory of his Battersea flat. As the owner of the Palm Centre at Richmond, West London, Martin Gibbons is one of Britain's leading palm experts, travelling the world in search of new and interesting species – especially those that are hardy in warmer parts of Britain.

Seven years ago he asked Jason Payne to redesign his garden. The brief was to provide privacy in an overlooked situation and to create a setting for his spectacular collection of palms and ferns. Payne was also asked to give the garden an oriental feel and to construct a pond that would reach wall to wall in this 5.5m (18ft) wide garden.

Payne is also interested in working with the sort of plants that the Palm Centre supplies. His aim here was to create a microcosm of exotic endangered woodland, providing a layered canopy of planting that is vertical, not horizontal, in structure. In seven years the garden has seen incredible growth and this has indeed provided a micro-climate for rarities. This garden can be seen as being a slice out of a densely planted forest environment.

Although the planting is the main subject, there is an understructure of hard landscaping. Moving from the house outwards, this consists of a raised terrace of black timber decking leading from the main living floor, which is raised above a sub-basement. Following the client's preference, this has a Chinese character with an upward curving pergola planted with trumpet vine (*Campsis radicans*). A staircase leads to ground level, where a winding gravel path set with paving slabs enters the jungle proper, curving in a large serpentine to the end of the site. The division between gravel and soil is made with an informal line of open textured gritstone that was chosen to patinate quickly.

PREVIOUS PAGES Many unusual hardy palms can be found growing in this garden. Here, the broad fan-shaped fronds of *Trachycarpus fortunii* make a dynamic display.

OPPOSITE Black stemmed bamboo (*Phyllostachys nigra*) frames one of the many vignettes along the winding gravel path, which makes the tour of the garden.

BELOW In a corner of the garden, ferns and palms mask the rectangular shape of the plot so that you can easily lose all sense of being in London. The perimeters of the garden hardly read in this dense, jungle-like planting.

The other major groundwork was the construction of the wide pond that entirely fills the end of the plot. The spoil from the excavation has been used to make a low mound on the north side of this east/west orientated garden. It is the sheer width of this pond that makes such a bold statement.

The best thing about this garden is the creativity of its planting. The tallest tree is a *Eucalyptus nitens*, which was planted when 46cm (1½ft) high seven years ago and has now reached 9m (30ft) tall. Other trees include a Monterey cypress, *Cupressus cashmeriana*, with attractive drooping grey/green foliage and Payne's favourite tree, the Santa Cruz ironwood tree (*Lyonothamnus floribundus* subsp. *aspleniifolius*) The latter is a tree he tries to incorporate in all his garden designs as it is very graceful, with fern-like evergreen leaves. It has a particularly slender habit so despite its height (it is already 8m/25ft) it is not an inappropriate tree for small gardens.

Moving down the canopy, the next layer is composed of several varieties of bamboo and it is these, more than anything, that provide the shelter for the rare palms that thrive in the garden. The entrance to the garden from the raised deck is framed by the dark outline of black bamboo (*Phyllostachys nigra*). Further along is a dense hedge-like clump of *Arundinaria nitida* and, beyond that, a bright gold stemmed clump of *Phyllostachys bambusoides* 'Holochrysa'. Recently these increasingly tall and shading bamboos were treated to Japanese pruning – they were halved in height, and the thinner stems removed to leave a sparser density of thick stems that will respond with a pom-pom of new growth.

The lower level is populated by a mixture of palms, ferns and low shrubs. Some of the palms are specimens that were grown from seeds collected by Martin Gibbons on his extensive plant hunting tours. He is particularly excited by high-altitude palms because they are potentially hardy in colder climates. In the Himalayas he discovered several new types of *Trachycarpus* and in his garden he has an example of the very rare *T. aureophilus*. Spread around the rest of the garden are *Chamaedorea microspadix* and

A walk around the garden becomes a mysterious exploration into unknown regions. The planting is layered as it is in a real jungle, with the different strata of foliage adapted to the light levels available.

Chamaedorea radicalis, relatives of the parlour palm, *Raphis excelsa*, as well as *Arenga engleri* from Taiwan. A particularly striking specimen is *Trithrinax acanthocoma*, which is 1.5m (5ft) high and has a spiked fibrous stem.

These palms have been cleverly combined with bold plantings of fern. For example, spreading on the hill is a scrambling fern, *Phymatasorus diversifolius*. There are some native ferns, such as common polypody (*Polypodium vulgare*) and harts tongue (*Asplenium scolopendriun*), but many more are exotic specimens, including the Tasmanian tree fern (*Dicksonia antarctica*) and *Polystichum proliferum*. A few low-growing shrubs complete the composition, such as *Olearia nummulariifolia*.

This garden stands out from most other urban gardens as a unique example of a complete exotic forest habitat. It is able, at the same time, to be both beautiful as well as provide the perfect growing environment for the plants it contains. It is also, with drip feed irrigation and just the occasional prune, virtually maintenance-free.

ABOVE At the furthest end of the garden an octagonal deck is cantilevered over a pool, which is the full width of the site. Foliage of different heights, habits and colours make up the composition. In the foreground the grey foliage of the often seen *Juniperus squamata* 'Blue Carpet' looks quite different in this context.

RIGHT The very fast growing silver top gum (*Eucalyptus nitens*) has grown to 9m (30ft) in seven years to form a striking vertical incident in the foreground of the garden.

BELOW Looking back towards the house you can appreciate how close to it the jungle actually encroaches. Everywhere tantalizing glimpses are framed by silhouetted stems that play an important part in the effect of the planting.

A Gothick Fantasy

St Johns Wood

Designer RUTH BARCLAY

Ruth Barclay sees her garden very much as a place for design experimentation. In the sixteen years she has lived in her charming pink 1830s Gothic-revival house, she has made some major revisions to the garden. The longer she gardens the more she feels she has to take radical decisions every few years, to keep the garden looking its best and to give it a fresh direction. Her aim for this garden has always been to have two outdoor rooms with different characters.

In common with many houses in the area, this property has a substantial front garden, and it is here that Ruth Barclay has made the more horticultural part of the garden. She wanted an exotic approach to the front door as well as a private oasis of green that can be viewed from the reception rooms. Although only a low wall protects this part of the garden from the street, considerable screening has been cleverly devised with planting: ivy is trained over an arch at the gate, and small trees and shrubs, such as *Magnolia* x *soulangeana* and camellia, break the line of the wall. This front garden is an intelligent mixture of the formal and the informal and reflects the late Regency period in style. It consists of a miniature central antiquarian parterre, box edging and box spiral topiary surrounded by a neat brick path and frilled ceramic edging. This is all contrasted against the surrounding beds of lush informal planting.

The much more private rear courtyard has a different feel; it is ordered and architectural. It is seen literally as an extension of the gothick conservatory Ruth Barclay and her husband built to link the house to a detached outbuilding. When the wide double doors of this conservatory are flung open it really does feel like one space, with the same white set with black tiled floor both inside and out. Only a few carefully chosen plants have been used here, and they are trained to conform to the overall scheme.

The main feature is a castellated iron canopy that houses a fountain mask set into a wall of lead scales. Strips of thin lead sheet, cut into zigzags, overlap to form a textured watery wall, and flanking mirrored panels cleverly dissolve the

ABOVE Dwarf rhododendrons bring
colour to the totally private front
garden. The bust of Beethoven in
the distance presides over a small
pool that can only be seen properly
from the dining room window.

LEFT The fountain forms the
viewstopper from the south-facing
conservatory in the rear garden.
It is framed by an iron canopy
planted with *Clematis armandii*.
The same paving is used in the
garden and the conservatory,
turning the two spaces into one
when the double doors are open.

boundary. This feature was designed by an architect friend,
Lionel Burgess: Ruth Barclay feels that an architectural
approach to the design of town gardens is essential to provide
a strong underlying geometric framework.

Mirrors are also used on the two walls to the east and
west of this small courtyard, contributing to the illusion of
space. They are set quite high on the wall and are framed by
perspective trelliswork, which is, at present, planted with a
frame of blue climbing solanum.

A number of architectural fragments and sculptures have
been integrated into the design to add interest. These vary
in size, from a near life-size classical figure to tiny fragments
on tables. Even the front garden has its hidden secrets – a
bust of Beethoven overlooks a tiny pool and rill.

This is a garden of jewel-like complexity. It is highly
controlled but still seems, in spite of this, to have an element
of jungly disordered growth. Such a successful compromise
can only be achieved with great attention to detail and a
periodic ruthless reassessment of the space.

A Dual-character Water Garden

Hackney

Designer JOHN TORDOFF

Although actor John Tordoff has lived in his 1860s Hackney house for twenty years, he only decided to address the garden twelve years ago. He attacked the problem of what to do with this large 25 x 8m (80 x 25ft) space in two phases. Initially, he decided to make a formal water garden next to the house, and only much later did he decide to treat the furthest part of the garden in a contrasting style. The theme that links the two areas is water, but it would be hard to treat the same element more differently. One half of the garden is geometrically organized in an Italian manner; the other half is inspired by Japan and is totally asymmetrical.

John Tordoff's philosophy of garden design is, he says, influenced by the theatre. His prime aim was to create a sense of mystery: to have a garden with a series of changing atmospheres that incorporates a surprise round every corner. He also wanted to make the walk round the garden as complicated as possible, with a lot of changes of direction and a series of symbolic references *en route*, so that it is a journey of alternating experiences. Although John Tordoff claims not to be a plantsman, he has devised a very inventive and successful mix of plants.

The first garden area leads off the basement sitting room and is enclosed by yew hedges. At its centre a stone-edged square pool has a Corinthian capital with a single fountain jet as its centrepiece. The surrounding paving slabs are diversified by a design of hard glazed encaustic tiles that John Tordoff found in the house and kept for later use. At each corner, box cubes provide the architectural frame for a series of symmetrically grouped plants, mostly in pots, although some are in small beds set into the paving. In the foreground a pair of variegated hollies (*Ilex* x *altaclerensis* 'Lawsoniana') are housed in baskets. Grey-foliaged plants are also used to great effect, such as topiarized *Cupressus arizonica* var. *glabra*, hosta and an *Argyranthemum frutescens*. The resulting colour contrasts come from foliage rather than flowers, though an arch frames the entrance to the second area and is trained with *Rosa* 'Maigold'.

The furthest part of this two-part
garden has a very different character
to the area that is nearest the house.
A hedge screens the two sections
from each other so that they are
quite separate entities.

LEFT Both azaleas and dwarf
rhododendron add colour to the
oriental garden, which has a green
and bright pink colour scheme.
It is filled with sculpture and
miniature architecture that give
an illusionistic scale to the garden.
These tiny details are discovered
by accident, rather than being
ostentatiously displayed.

BELOW Baby's tears (*Soleirolia
soleirolii*) takes the place of grass,
and, because it needs no mowing,
can accommodate complex contours.
The landscape illusion is aided by the
use of dwarf trees and shrubs planted
in this green sward.

Once through the arch, you enter a totally different world.
This garden contains a whole series of elements derived
from China and Japan. The main feature is made up of
a meandering rill flanked by humpy mounds of baby's
tears (*Soleirolia soleirolii*). This plant takes the place
of grass but, because its dense form needs no cutting, it
has been possible to use it to create a sort of 'miniature
landscape' with contours. The exact size of this landscape is
hard to appreciate. Is it a large river winding through hills,
or a tiny stream in a narrow cutting? This duality of scale is
cleverly played up by the scattering of miniature temples
and pagodas across the scene. These contrast with the life-
size tea house that is raised on stilts to give a bird's eye view
across the garden. Gnarled rocks, some of them broken
pieces of concrete found in skips, could be giant geological
formations or the carefully chosen stones of a Zen garden.

The planting is a diverse mixture of dwarf conifers, small
azaleas and rhododendrons, shuttlecock ferns and a swathe
of wisteria on suspended bamboo screening. The latter
forms a sort of proscenium frame to this magically theatrical
and exotic set piece. It is a truly remarkable garden.

ABOVE This theatrical property – a crown used in a production that the owner of the garden appeared in – has been casually left on a cushion of box: one of the many small details that enrich the garden.

RIGHT Miniature Chinese buildings and fences have been placed in an improvised rocky landscape of broken concrete chunks and are combined with dwarf conifers. This might easily have degenerated into model village kitsch but it doesn't, mainly because of the strong design carried throughout the landscape.

A Mountain Retreat

Notting Hill

Designer TOM VACH

ABOVE This artificial mountain side of Northumberland slate has been diversified in places with pebbles. Baby's tears (*Soleirolia soleirolii*), a useful substitute for grass in London gardens where mowing isn't an option, has been used as the unifying ground cover.

OPPOSITE It is the boldness of the concept of this artificial rock face that makes it so successful. It has the scale of Victorian Pulhamite rockwork – artificial rockwork designed on a bold scale from the now defunct Pulham's Works – quite unlike the paltry effect of many modern rockeries.

This amazing alpine landscape, which is in the tradition of nineteenth-century artificial rockwork, has been created by Tom Vach, the man behind the fashionable London florists 'Harper and Tom's'. Tom Vach didn't 'discover' flowers and gardening until he was in his mid-forties, but his eye for design and taste for wild landscapes have inspired his subsequent career. He constructed this complex strata of Northumbrian slate for a variety of reasons – partly to link his small sunken garden with the communal gardens that are 3m (10ft) higher than his own 12 x 6m (40 x 20ft) plot, but also to recreate the mountainous landscapes he loves.

The problem he was presented with when he first moved here was the 'bombsite' left by the previous occupants who had also tried to resolve this difficult sunken site. Tom Vach toyed with two or three schemes, all involving tiered steps or stages to retain the vast and steep wall of soil already in place. The two schemes he rejected employed more geometric solutions – one interlocked terraced squares of brick, the other was a composition of circular stair treads with the feel of a Busby Berkley film set. The final, more naturalistic, solution retains this illusionistic quality, and the garden can be seen as an outdoor theatre, with its series of changing effects reflecting the seasons.

The exact topographical location of the garden is not important; at certain times the rock face can be reminiscent of Cornwall, the Alps or, when it snows, even Mount Kilimanjaro! The hard landscaping, which is made up of a central valley flanked by steeper banks, is punctuated with soil pockets that provide a framework for a wide variety of plants. This is not a conventional garden of alpines, but accommodates such diverse subjects as bamboo, tree ferns, baby's tears and *Alchemilla mollis*, along with smaller, more conventional rockery pinks and harebells. The planting has been carefully designed to ensure there is something of interest all year round. Colour combinations are largely confined to pink, blue and white – Tom Vach particularly likes magenta pink, as it goes so well with slate grey.

The landscape is divided broadly into Mediterranean plants on the left, an 'orchard and meadow' on the right, and 'woodland' backing onto the trees of the communal garden. At the very top is a pool. But these divisions are notional rather than rigid. The Mediterranean ridge is covered with herbs: thyme, rosemary, sage and lavender, but these are mixed with the large foliage of acanthus and cardoon. The 'woodland' is composed of an exotic mix of oleander, azalea and rhododendrons backed by the dense foliage of bamboo, bay and tree fern. In the summer *Alchemilla mollis* and white lavatera make a show on the Orchard Hill. During this season, Tom Vach often leaves the hose running out of the pond to cause a spectacular, large scale cascade, which runs the full height of the slate 'steps'.

A very small space right beside the house has become a terrace, just large enough for a small table and four chairs. This is designed to make the transition from the modern interior out into the 'wild' landscape.

This garden, like many in London, is both exotic and theatrical. The hard landscaping was conceived as a stage backdrop for the planting and the whole scene is totally private, designed to be seen from the basement sitting room's wide, oriental-looking, double doors. The resulting illusion of being far from Notting Hill is astonishing.

RIGHT The pool at the head of the 'valley' provides scope for a further composition of driftwood and pebbles. At the very back of the site, ferns and bamboo form the division between the rockwork and the communal garden beyond.

BELOW The purple-black of the grass-like *Ophiopogon planiscapus* 'Nigrescens', the green of *Alchemilla mollis* (one of the owner's favourite plants) and baby's tears go well with slate grey. These plants colonize the fissures – the 'beds' of this garden.

Lush Garden Rooms

Chelsea

Designer MALCOLM HILLIER

Garden designer and writer of books on flowers, gardens and cookery, Malcolm Hillier has lived in his present London house for twelve years. The design he formulated for the garden as soon as he moved in has largely been executed as planned, though some of the detail has evolved as inspiration struck or plants and objects suggested themselves. Malcolm Hillier is a knowledgeable plantsman and he also gardens in the West Indies; there is a noticeable degree of lush, opulent planting in his Chelsea garden, redolent of the tropics. The plot (about 35m/115ft long) has been divided into a series of layers of different character, partly determined by the fact that the house faces north, making the sunken area immediately adjacent to the kitchen permanently shaded. About three quarters of the area beyond the shade of the tall house is sunny. There is also, very unusually for this dense area of London, a sunny 9m (30ft) front garden.

The whole idea of the garden was to make it appeal to all the senses. This fits in nicely with the seventeenth-century house; at the time it was built, gardens were arranged to delight the eye, be rich in scent, full of delicious fruits, to encompass the sound of water and, at the same time, appeal to the intellect. Malcom Hillier has composed a modern update of this notion. Although, originally, there was a pleasant garden in place, hardly anything of that layout remains except for a morello cherry and a crab apple.

The shaded sunken terrace nearest to the house is the most 'room-like' part of the garden. It is largely paved with a random mix of old York stone and slate. Rising out of an oblong pool, the brick wall has been painted with a pink earth-pigmented limewash to visually warm up this shady area. The space is defined by a cedar pergola with a copper capping planted with *Aristolochia* and white *Chaenomeles speciosa* 'Nivalis'. Tree ferns, hostas and pyracantha also flourish in the dense shade – Malcolm Hillier has been devoted to tree ferns since the 1960s and is pleased that they now have a much more universal appeal.

A formal pool at the shaded house
end of the garden is populated by fish.
For their sake, a glass float stops the
pool from freezing over completely
in hard winters.

From this terrace area, a flight of steps leads up to the rest of the garden, which consists of a series of layers divided by hedges and culminating in a pergola of Tuscan columns at the sunny end of the garden. Here 3m (9ft) walls are topped by a further 3m (9ft) of trellis to make a perfectly secluded and sheltered place where deliciously scented but tender climbers such as *Trachelospermum jasminoides* and *Dregea sinensis* can flourish. *Rosa* 'New Dawn' also combines its scent with *Jasminum beesianum*, making this corner fantastically sweet-smelling. The walk through the hedged enclosures is linked by a herringbone path consisting of specially made bricks. Throughout the garden great attention has been paid to such details and to the quality of surfaces and materials.

The 'taste' element of the garden is supplied by cherries, crab apples, pears and herbs that are spread throughout the area, rather than concentrated in one place. This is a garden of very disparate planting, but it is all held together by an ordered geometry and an eye that carefully controls the lush effects. You get the sense that the seventeenth-century owners of this house would have approved of this updated garden. It is very international in flavour, and can be seen to represent a microcosm of the world's flora.

An Indian Rooftop

Chelsea

Designer MARTIN SUMMERS

When Martin Summers and his family moved into this Chelsea artist's studio more than twenty years ago they felt the lack of a garden deeply and decided to colonize the only outdoor space available – the complex roof area of this late nineteenth-century building. What has developed over the years is a fantastic and highly amusing recreation of Eastern exoticism. There is so much going on within the relatively confined space that visitors find themselves constantly surprised by the plants and objects hidden in nooks and crannies. The garden is so successful that Martin Summers now designs a range of garden effects for others.

As an art dealer he travels extensively, and always brings back an interesting piece of sculpture, a pot or an object that inevitably finds its way onto the roof. The overall effect this has had on the space has been to make it into a rich, tropical landscape – though, paradoxically, the plants that conjure up this illusion are largely European.

The structural features of the garden were determined many years ago when 5m (15ft) minarets were bought. They set the tone for the style of the garden, which has gradually been intensified and elaborated on year by year. The approach to the garden, a series of narrow alleys between walls, has been made into an exciting experience by inventive use of mirror-backed trellis hung with pots that by night are mysteriously lit. Being a studio, most of the house is one storey tall with large skylights that, from below, give you tantalizing glimpses of the garden. The one room that has a conventional view of the garden is the bedroom. From all the windows there are spectacular views at night when the garden is cunningly lit from forty different sources.

The planting on the roof has multiplied and there are now some 2000 pots filled with various types of plants. Everything, apart from ivies that come up from ground level, is grown in these containers, which range from small hanging Javanese pots through to large wooden tubs. The pots are rearranged to suit different times of year – so a camellia might be brought forward in spring, and pushed

On this Chelsea roof, resin casts of minarets from the Brighton Pavilion set the oriental tone of the scheme. This is reinforced throughout the garden by miniature eastern scenes, such as the pagoda in the foreground of the picture.

back to become background foliage for the rest of the year. Every season vast numbers of fuchsia are potted up; their hot pink flowers add an Indian palette to the greenery. There are also luridly coloured bedding plants such as *Impatiens walleriana* (Busy Lizzie), which give a long season of appropriately oriental lacquer red. All of this has to be watered in summer by hand; a task many gardener's view as a relaxing ritual.

The route round the garden, on decking walkways, takes in a vast range of still-life compositions of buddhas, oriental sculptures of many kinds and a miniature Crystal Palace, peopled by articulated dolls specially made as portraits of Martin Summers and his family. This contains a complete indoor garden that is the only part of the garden to be automatically irrigated. This deeply eccentric folly delightfully encapsulates the whole tone of the garden, which has a dream-like unreality to it. You can hardly believe that this garden exists where it does, or that such a private elysium has been created in the centre of London.

ABOVE Raised walkways direct the tour of the garden through the different roof levels. Every plant is grown in a container, including some quite large trees, such as the false acacia (*Robinia pseudoacacia*) on the left.

RIGHT An oriental stone bust is framed by fuschias. This particular flower is favoured by the owner both for its long reliable flowering season and its wide range of hot Indian pinks.

BELOW Large scale bronze cranes perch on the rooftop. The garden is lit at night from a variety of sources, and the minarets are wired for both light and sound – one of the delights being a tape of country bird songs.

ABOVE Hanging Javanese pots are
planted with ferns. The ivies that
grow behind them are the only plants
to be planted in soil at ground level.
They climb their way to the roof,
where they clothe the boundary trellis.

RIGHT Here another Eastern
composition is made from a variety
of fuschias, miniature roses, hebes,
sweet peas and pansies. Martin
Summers conjures up his oriental
fantasy with a variety of plant
material; most of the flowering
part is renewed each season.

Natural

Two Gardens into One

Hackney

Designer DAVID FRENCH

It is very rare that two London neighbours get on so well that they decide to collaborate on a joint project. In this instance architect David French and his neighbours Fiona and Sandy MacLennan, who are textile design consultants, decided that their gardens would benefit from an element of mutuality.

Their very simple idea was to link the two gardens at the furthest ends by building a gazebo actually on the dividing line. This meant demolishing part of the old brick wall that separates the gardens, but was worth doing as they gained so much visual space. Opening up space in this way is a concept that many friendly neighbours should consider.

David French designed the gazebo so that it could easily be divided down the middle into two separate parts, accessed from each side should either, or both, the owners move. But for the present, the building forms an actual and visual link between the two spaces. It has been conceived as an early nineteenth-century gothick greenhouse, and was constructed out of timber with a lead roof. The woodwork is painted a blue/grey; an excellent foil to the brighter greens of foliage and, incidentally, a colour the innovative early twentieth-century garden designer Gertrude Jekyll approved of for garden structures. It was called by her French blue – a colour she noted as being much seen in France and Italy on painted woodwork. Used on trellis and garden buildings, this colour defines the structure without making it appear to jump forward, or without competing with the greens of foliage (which is what brighter shades unfortunately often do).

The gazebo has a number of effects on the flanking gardens. Firstly its height adds apparent width to both, which are of the standard elongated oblong form of most London plots. Secondly, because the building is glazed and has doors on both sides, it opens up wide lateral vistas across both sites so that each enjoys a borrowed view of the other.

Apart from this one link, the two gardens are quite distinct in style. Being an architect, David French has designed his garden on a geometric plan, although he readily admits he only really got to grips with it after the

PREVIOUS PAGES The gothick pavilion on the left is shared by two adjacent gardens, and forms the centrepiece of both. On David French's side, shown here, a wirework conical plant support is painted the same dull grey/blue as the pavilion; this colour makes a satisfactory foil for the greens of foliage.

RIGHT The pavilion is accessed from both gardens and, close to it, a gilded dolphin fountain designed by David French against a Lutyens-style brick and tile niche, brings the soothing sound of water within earshot.

BELOW On the lower terrace, near to David French's house, a warm terracotta colour scheme dominates. Terracotta balls make a still-life composition with large Italian pots planted with evergreens against quarry tiled paving.

MacLennans moved in next door, ten years after him. He was inspired by their speedy efforts to transform their own space. Their initial idea to build a pavilion appealed to him as he wanted to replace an unaesthetic shed.

David French's garden is composed of a series of interlocking ellipses that divide the area into three separate sections. The geometry has been softened in the twelve years since it was originally created by maturing planting. His aim was to create a series of different views so that there is a variety of interest wherever you are in the garden. Each vignette is supplied with a viewstopping object, ranging in complexity from terracotta balls to a gilded bronze dolphin, which is the culmination of the whole composition. Near to the house a clay-tiled terrace is covered with pots, and this terrace has steps up to the main level of the garden. Mop-headed *Ligustrum delavayanum* and clipped box balls make a formal contrast against the generally informal planting. The enclosing walls have been softened and dissolved with climbing plants: jasmine, ivy and clematis, making it impossible to determine quite how big the garden is – it is actually 22 x 8m (72 x 25ft).

A rather *ad hoc* approach to purchases – plants were bought individually as they were found in the local market, rather than being items in a great master plan – has worked because they have been rather left to their own devices, and ramble naturally one into another. However, there is an overall controlling eye, making thoughtful juxtapositions of leaf shape, texture and foliage colour throughout the space.

Almost every London garden benefits in some way from its neighbour – whether it be a formal garden set against an informal one, or a garden that benefits from the larger background of trees and shrubs that can be found next door. However, this particular garden is a model of the very American approach where plots merge imperceptively into each other with seemingly no visible boundaries. An overall enlargement of scale and broadness of effect is the pleasing consequence.

A raised box-edged terrace at one end of the garden makes a sunny place to sit. In the foreground alstroemeria, euphorbia and variegated hebes and hollies form part of the eclectic planting scheme.

A Vibrant Coloured Rooftop

Brixton

Designers MICHAEL CLARK & SIMON STEELE

Michael Clark and Simon Steele live in the flat below this roof, which consists of an area approximately 5 x 14m (15 x 45ft). Their colonization of it has been so successful that the neighbours have been inspired to garden their own adjacent roof spaces. It is a very exposed place open to both sun and wind but, with bamboo windscreening and constant attention to watering, the designers have been able to create a lush and fertile garden. Keen gardeners, they also work an allotment nearby. However, it is above all their flair for colour and composition, which has ensured the success of their cultivation of this somewhat inhospitable rooftop space. In the wrong hands, the overall idea could easily have rapidly turned into an uncoordinated mess, but this roof garden has become a magnificent feast of colour and imagination.

The main architectural feature of most flat roofs, the chimney stack, has been turned here into one of the main elements of the garden's composition by being painted a wonderful distressed blue. This one strong feature holds the rest of the disparate plan together visually. It has been painted in artist's acrylic with a PVA glaze. The paint was applied thinly so that the light basecoat shows through, giving the blue a remarkable luminous quality that works especially well at night.

The design of this garden has grown organically rather than on the basis of a set plan. All the plants are grown in pots or containers of various sorts and plants have been added bit by bit as they, or their pots, have been discovered. One of the joys of the garden is the very mixed collection of containers that have just been found. These range from old damaged builder's buckets, fruit baskets abandoned by nearby market stalls, tin baths to leaky watering cans – all these have been filled with compost and planted up (the fruit baskets having first been lined with black polythene).

This *ad hoc* approach has also extended to the planting where any haphazard arrival from elsewhere has been welcomed. Fennel and valerian, for instance, appeared from the ether – they were not planted. The planting is deliberately

LEFT On this roof terrace, bold blocks of vibrant colour hold the composition of disparate planting together. Selected fruit and vegetables have migrated from an allotment onto this roof.

BELOW The foliage and flower heads of cardoon (*Cynara cardunculus*) make a big impact, showing up especially well against the bright blue wash of artist's acrylic on the wall of the roof's access hatch.

LEFT A galvanized tin tub makes a
good environment for water plants,
including snake grass, mint and
the corkscrewed *Juncus effusus*
'Spiralis'. Metal floats give the
ensemble a sculptural quality
and help to slow down the freezing
process in winter.

BELOW The largest tree on the roof,
a silver birch, was planted small
seven years ago but now makes a
substantial impact on the garden.
Bamboo screens act as a windbreak
and also provide privacy.

mixed: there are large groups of bamboos and grasses, vegetables, herbaceous plants, trees and shrubs. One of the oldest trees, a silver birch planted in a 1m (3ft) square purpose-made container as a tiny sapling seven years ago, has turned into a large handsome specimen that gives height to a corner of the garden. The containers are grouped as they might be in a border to create broad masses of varied height and texture. The beauty of using pots for planting means that there can be juxtapositions of certain plants that would not work if they were competing in the same soil. It also means that they can be rearranged at will to create different groupings according to the season.

Some of the vegetables that can be grown in pots have migrated from the allotment to this garden for easy picking and proximity to the kitchen. These include tomatoes, peppers, runner beans, and yellow courgettes. There are also fruit trees, and a conference pear planted in 35cm (14in) clay pots, which crop excellently. Some of the larger ornamental herbs also bring bold scale to the plant groupings: fennel, valerian and tansy among them. Giants such as cardoon and *Lobelia cardinalis* further diversify the overall scale of the garden.

This rooftop space is used particularly on balmy summer nights, and this, so the owners say, is when it is at its best. The orange glow from the nearby street lights give it a warm cast that is supplemented by the light of many hurricane lamps and night lights placed in jam jars; these may be a cheap substitute for Vauxhall lights, but they provides just as good an effect.

The garden is full of invention and a delightful 'make-do-and-mend' aesthetic. A portable lawn on wheels was made for the dog by fixing 15 x 2.5cm (6 x 1in) boards around a wheeled platform given by a neighbour. Brightly coloured canvas deckchairs have been added to extend the overall colour palette used. These also provide an extra element to the compositional possibilities and make an especially big impact in summer.

Some exotic plants survive outside all year round in this well heated micro-climate. Agaves stay outside through winter without suffering, but others, like the *Brugmansia* that was forgotten one winter season, occasionally suffer. Generally, though, this is a very warm spot, where plants thrive in nurturing conditions. There are 182 pots on the roof, all watered by hand daily in the summer. Before a stand pipe was installed this was done by carrying cans from downstairs – now the plants are watered by hose, although it still takes ages, as anyone with a collection of pot plants will know.

The great thing about growing plants in pots is that you are not restricted at all and can experiment with species that like different conditions and soil types. Here, water plants have been placed in a miniature pond (actually an old tin bath); the striped snake grass making a pleasing composition with metal fishermen's floats. Luxuriant displays of hosta are contrived even in this hot sunny space. The entire garden is a monument to what good husbandry can achieve in less than perfect conditions. It is certainly an excellent illustration of how an artistic eye can turn a disparate collection of plants and objects into a highly successful, unified and aesthetic whole.

Plants are massed together as if in a large border, graded by height and organized by habit and texture. No particular distinction is made between fruit, flower, vegetable or herb – all are mixed together for the overall visual effect.

A Composer's Hidden Garden

Islington

Designer MICHELE OSBORNE

When composer Michael Nyman wanted his new Islington garden redesigned two years ago he asked an old friend, Michèle Osborne, to recreate the space as quickly as she could. He wanted an element of privacy but did not like the overgrown, oppressive planting of the existing garden. Osborne was required to open the garden up on the one hand but to give a greater sense of seclusion and privacy on the other – instructions seemingly at odds with each other, but cleverly reconciled by this inventive designer.

The first requirement was achieved by clearing all the overgrowth. This freed up two large planting spaces with sunny and shady parts, which provided varied growing conditions. Privacy was ensured by adding woven willow trellis to the top of the low brick walls, almost doubling their height. The trellis was then densely planted with roses, clematis, solanum and Virginia creeper to give a textured backdrop to the garden and to soften the boundaries.

The predominant colour in the garden is provided by the various greens of the carefully selected foliage. Flowers are in a muted palette of white, faded purple, pink and blue, which makes for a supremely restful effect without the jarring brilliance of fashionable orange, yellow and red. It is interesting to note that hardly any London gardens use the hot colour range because, in a small space, it can become oppressively violent. Such colours visually jump forward, making a confined space appear even more so. What works in a country garden, where there is distance and insulation of one part from another, rarely succeeds in an urban space, except where exotic colour cacophony is the aim.

In this garden there is no such harshness. The colours of the hard landscaping: Yorkstone, grey London brick, and stone retaining walls, continue the subtle effect with the patina of natural materials. Only the white iron furniture and black iron rose arch add a graphic element to the design. The levels and retaining walls of the existing garden were kept, but the paving was relaid and the steps into the garden were widened to give a better approach from the house.

RIGHT This unusual assemblage, devised by Michael Nyman, provides a focal point to the garden. The mirrored back of the cabinet catches the eye because it reflects light. On top of it is a wirework torso that was purchased in Los Angeles.

BELOW *Solanum jasminoides* cascades down from woven willow trellis that is fixed above a low wall. This plant lightens the effect of the ferns on the shaded side of the garden.

The planting was designed to provide contrasting shape and texture. Ferns, euphorbias and hellebores flourish in the shadier parts of the garden. Lavender, an olive tree, roses and herbs enjoy the sunny side. The paved areas are broken up with pots of geranium and herbs, with box balls in pots adding year-round effect, flanking the entrance to the circular terrace at the centre of the garden. As an enthusiastic cook Michael Nyman is particularly keen on the varied herbs that the garden contains. The paved terrace is used as often as possible as an outdoor dining room.

Viewed from this terrace, the focal point of the garden is a delightfully surreal assemblage consisting of a mirror-backed display cabinet that is used as a plinth to display an antique wirework torso that was bought by Michael Nyman in Los Angeles. Backed by luxuriant Virginia creeper, this viewstopper gives the garden a rather dream-like air that is reminiscent of a Dali or a Leonora Carrington landscape. An appropriate place for this intensely creative artist to think about his own compositions.

LEFT The hard landscaping was reworked by the designer and new retaining walls were built from old stone cobbles. The advantage of raised beds, particularly surrounding seating areas, is that the planting can be brought much more within the field of vision.

BELOW There are no harsh colours in this scheme at all. Soft pink, blue and purple – composed here of lavender, geranium, buddleia, aquilegia and roses – predominate throughout the garden.

Rus in Urbe

Hackney

Designer ROSE COOPER

Rose Cooper's garden in Hackney is of the sort you might expect to find around a Regency *cottage ornée* in the country. It is a very clever confection of objects and planting, all of which go perfectly with her early nineteenth-century house. Her aim was to create a completely private enclosed garden that is both cottagey and stylish.

There is a strong gothick element in this garden. Rose Cooper's taste is for the rather whimsical gothick that was in fashion before the more accurately antiquarian Gothic style of the mid nineteenth century. Clever use has been made here of architectural salvage to create structure in the garden. The tone is set by an arbour, a cast iron gothick window, white gothick chairs and a modern gothick planter. There are other, more subtle suggestions of the style – four scallop shells arranged in a terracotta dish of water are reminiscent of Pilgrim's badges, wrought iron scrolled finials have been placed within a border, and piles of damaged decorative masonry all reinforce the image of an early nineteenth-century picturesque scene.

The feeling of enclosure has been achieved by the lush planting of the walls and the house with climbers – mainly roses and clematis – alongside an opulent planting of the surrounding borders with tall perennials. The use of colour has been carefully modulated to include only blue, pink and white in the main garden, with blue and yellow in the front.

The main lawn has a delightful centrepiece composed of an octagonal jardiniere planted up in summer with grey and white; *Argyranthemum frutescens*, white verbena and petunia and trailing *Helichrysum*. This central feature is surrounded by eight large clipped box balls in terracotta pots that give an air of age and permanence to the garden. Accents of white, both in objects and planting, have been used throughout the garden to lighten the overall effect of this relatively shady, predominantly green space.

There are innumerable small details in this garden that visitors can come across more or less by chance, such as the imaginative still-life arrangements of found objects

It is hard to imagine that this cosy garden is to be found in the densely populated area of Hackney. Regency gothick is the *leitmotif* of the garden, and references to the style can be found throughout.

skillfully combined with low plantings of ferns and ground cover. Still-life compositions are also made from the many pot-grown plants in the garden, which include agapanthus, hosta, viola and topiarized box.

The apparently casual air of the planting in this garden has in fact been achieved by careful organization, and the permitting of a certain, carefully monitored, amount of rampant growth. This is noticeable where climbers clothe structures. The effect would be lost if too much of the supporting structure were covered up and yet here, although the climbers are controlled, you still get the sense of natural growth. The effect of the planting is heightened by the juxtaposition of light shades with dark; grey and silver foliage is cleverly interspersed with darker greens.

A light, sunny terrace, perfect for outdoor meals, is furnished with a nineteenth-century French table and chairs in red oxide-painted ironwork. This is one of the hottest colours in the garden, but it is saved from striking a jarring note by its old pitted surface. Indeed, this is a garden with a great feeling of maturity, which is a result of the designer's feeling for the patina of surface and her sensitivity to texture in planting. All of this, combined with the sense of mystery added by the framed entrances to different parts of the garden, creates the sense of private intimacy that is its overall dominant mood.

Recreated Afresh

Notting Hill

Designer KIM WHATMORE

Jean Ross Russell and her family have lived in this Notting Hill house for thirty years, during which time they have often recreated the garden. Recently, they commissioned Kim Whatmore to reinvent the garden yet again and to tidy up the parts of it that they had never found satisfactory. Jean Ross Russell wanted a garden with structure, softened by lush planting that would have year-round effect. She wanted to retain some of her favourite plants and to reuse the existing Gothic arches that had previously been arranged as a linked-up circular arbour in the centre of the garden. Her friends, she says, had always thought this a mad configuration in a garden only 6 x 15m (20 x 50ft). However, such a bold statement of this sort does often work better in a small garden than would a series of less confident, smaller scale effects.

Whatmore took some of the existing features and then rearranged them to make a very different composition. The ground surfaces are now largely paved in various materials and she has added a large decking terrace that links the ground floor door (1m/3ft above soil level) to the garden proper. This has made access to the garden much easier, and also links the house to the garden visually in a way that had been missing before. From the door three fan-shaped steps lead to a large deck, 6 x 5m (20 x 15ft). This area is now a warm and clean platform – much more inviting to step onto with bare feet than a cold paving slab or wet grass.

A further three steps, also of timber, descend to the main part of the garden; their curved shape echoes the key geometrical feature of the garden – a large central circular space defined by radiating brickwork and filled with large river-washed pebbles. This focal point contains three objects of interest: a low bubbling fountain, two sculptures of small children, and an already existing, handsome specimen of *Acer japonicum* 'Vitifolium'. Planting within the pebbled circle has been left sparse so that the main elements are not obscured, but at different times of the year small incidents enliven it – such as tiny white cyclamen, lungwort and small-leaved iris.

This garden has been devised to have an interesting effect throughout the year. Here, autumn foliage colour is supplemented by late roses. The strong pattern of the paving and the light, Gothic-shaped arches come into their own in winter.

ABOVE The central pebble circle has
been sparsely planted with cyclamen,
lungwort, hostas and iris. In the
autumn, the variously coloured fallen
leaves of *Acer japonicum* 'Vitifolium'
add temporary spots of jewel-like
colour to this area.

LEFT The metal arches were recycled
from an earlier scheme – they now
provide a series of screens projecting
into the garden from the side walls.
They are all symmetrically positioned,
but have been planted up differently.

Four of the existing Gothic arches have been resited to form
screens, coming out into the garden from the side walls at
right angles. These help to give the garden spatial interest
by creating layers and, as they are clothed with climbers,
they give height without forming solid walls of foliage. The
rest of the ground surface is covered with York stone that
has been left ungrouted to provide places for random
plantings. These are the substitutes for proper beds, which
have largely been eliminated. At the moment, the areas
contain self-seeded chamomile, hostas and mint.

The garden was designed to have flowering interest all
year and the colours have been restricted to pink, white and
blue/purple. For example, in spring, tulips, polyanthus
and wallflowers at the lower level are accompanied by early
clematis higher up. However, in winter, the geometry of the
layout really comes into its own; this is especially stunning
when viewed from the upper rooms of the four storey house.

Three seats at the lower level face north, east and west
and offer vantage points in a garden that has been designed
to look good from all angles. This recreated space is an
inspiration to anyone wanting to give their garden a face lift.

Formal

A Topiary Garden

Kennington

Designer ANDREW DICKERSON

When the art dealer Andrew Dickerson and his family moved into this late eighteenth-century Kennington house twelve years ago, only the walls of the garden existed. He has now brought his own taste for abstract composition to this modern reinterpretation of the topiary garden.

Although the design seems on the surface very like a late seventeenth-century or early eighteenth-century formal garden, it does have some interesting differences. Despite having a symmetrical central axis, it is not a symmetrical garden. The intention of the garden is also fundamentally different – during the seventeenth century geometric perfection was the ideal, and the closer plants could be trained into perfect cones, pyramids or spheres the better. Andrew Dickerson, however, admires the irregular forms of old topiary – the sort to be found in churchyards or flanking cottage doors. He likes the idea that the plant, though clipped, is allowed to find its own shape to some extent, so that each has a slightly different character. This has lent quirkiness and individuality to the garden, which, as the years go by, will become more and more pronounced. The analogy he uses is his own children; he has tried to form them but they will inevitably turn into their own people – perhaps not as he might have expected, but they will be just as loveable.

The whole garden design is carried out largely in yew and box. The perimeter walls are covered in yew hedging to a height of about 2m (6ft). The end wall is hidden by a curved yew hedge that would have been called an 'exedra' by the eighteenth-century landscape gardener William Kent, copies of whose urns decorate the garden. The exedral form was much used in neo-Palladian gardens as a setting for antique statuary or, as found here, simply for its pleasing architectural curve.

One of the many pleasures of this sort of garden is the play of light on the sculptural forms and the shadows that they cast. These are particularly effective when the sun is low in the morning or evening. The garden also looks great

PREVIOUS PAGES Although the experience of the changing seasons in a garden of evergreens is more subtle than it is in a garden of flowers, it is no less pleasurable. For example, the lingering frost on grass and topiary here enlivens the composition.

BELOW From above one can appreciate the geometry of the layout of formal gardens that may not be apparent at ground level. Although it has a central axis, this garden also has important diagonal vistas by virtue of the off-axis placing of urns and other key elements.

in frost or by moonlight. It is not artificially lit, except for a halogen spot on the terrace that faces the garden, making it eerily unreal and flat-looking – almost like a stage set made of pasteboard. It is possibly this theatrical element that makes the garden popular with children – it is certainly an excellent place for a game of 'hide-and-seek'.

The garden is deliberately designed to look good from above, from where the clarity of its ground plan is especially effective. The Dickersons are particularly lucky because the trees of the surrounding gardens add a mature backdrop to the scene – there are fine specimens of mulberry, pear and gleditsia. As Andrew Dickerson says, '... it would be awful if all the neighbours' gardens were like ours, but we benefit from the contrasting, informal background.'

Looking into the garden from the house, the foreground is defined by a York stone paved terrace into which box cones and standard bay are set. There are also classical Italian terracotta pots with festoons in relief; some planted with box balls, others with white agapanthus or white

ABOVE From seat level on the terrace, the topiary shapes make ever changing sculptural compositions. Some are planted in spaces left in the York stone, while others have been placed in large terracotta pots.

LEFT Unlike most topiary gardens this one is deliberately unsymmetrical. The owner also takes great delight in the slightly wayward shapes that the cones, pyramids and spheres are allowed to follow.

tulips – these, apart from a small lavender hedge, are the only concession to flowers. The rest of the garden's surface is made up of closely cut lawn.

The maintenance of the garden is not high – it is a fallacy that formal gardens are automatically labour intensive. Apart from cutting the grass, Andrew Dickerson trims the box and yew twice a year, though he likes to do this when the mood takes him rather than blitzing the garden at regular set times. He finds the occasional clipping to be a restful break from his work.

The two William Kent urns have been placed carefully, in order to heighten the perspectival recession of the site. One has been put in the middle ground on the right; the other in the distance on the left. Andrew Dickerson has taken great trouble to encourage these urns to patinate with moss and lichen and, despite protestations from friends that the London atmosphere is too polluted to grow lichens, he has succeeded. It is the patina of age that is found on gravestones that he would like to encourage. This is another reference to churchyards, which partly inspired the garden. Indeed, he has cleverly reproduced the same sort of atmosphere in this very still and restful garden, which, from every angle, produces new and delightful compositions.

Formality and Informality

Chelsea

Designer MARGY FENWICK

When Margy Fenwick and her husband bought their London house ten years ago there was nothing in the garden at all – just a mature backcloth of trees in the surrounding gardens. It was partly the open space in this densely packed part of Chelsea that attracted them to the house.

Margy Fenwick sees the garden very much as an outdoor room – perhaps even the most important room of the house. She is attracted to gardening because of its permanence. In interiors and clothes, fashions come and go season by season. But in gardens there is continuity.

The layout of the house and the routes into the garden were changed at the same time and the garden is now approached by a staircase from the drawing room floor above and from the basement kitchen below. The garden is very much designed with a bird's eye view in mind and exciting perspectives are to be had from the upper floors of this tall house.

Having engaged the garden much more with the house, Margy Fenwick set about making a real outdoor dining room at the far end of it, on a slightly raised, paved platform. She commissioned Matthew Eden, the master of garden wire and metalwork, to make an elegant metal arbour the full width of the garden. Climbers have been trained over this to give it both a living roof and dappled shade. The major part of the arbour is covered in *Clematis armandii*, whose white flowers are anxiously awaited every spring when they form a white dome that totally electrifies the scene. The roof shape for the arbour was taken from the 1840s Palm House at Kew, but its overall form is also reminiscent of the carpenters' work arbours that are prevalent in Italian Renaissance paintings.

The whole garden has an Italian feel, with little box parterres, topiary and a central fountain. The box edged beds are, however, not conventional parterres, but are planted up with box and *Ligustrum delavayanum* mopheads that, at different times of year, are diversified by plantings of white tulips in spring, white lilies ('Casablanca')

RIGHT Designed to be seen from above, when you view this garden from the drawing room you can really appreciate the layout. The box hedges are redefined each spring with a fresh sprinkling of pea gravel to give a visually sharper effect.

BELOW This Chelsea garden has a strictly white and green colour scheme. The spring planting includes white hyacinths and primulas.

in summer and white Japanese anemones in autumn. Brighter, fashionable, colours have been experimented with but these have always been found to be unsatisfactory and the garden has reverted to the preferred green and white scheme. This is such a successful formula in the confined space of London gardens that many chose its restful effect in preference to any other colour scheme.

One of the many inventive aspects of this garden is the way the edges of the box hedging are given definition with a narrow band of pea gravel between the hedge and the York stone paving. This is particularly effective when viewed from above where it helps to sharpen the geometry of the overall layout. The same technique was used in the seventeenth and early eighteenth century when parterres were usually surrounded by narrow bands of sand or gravel. These box-edged beds give the illusion of symmetry to the garden, even though they themselves are not actually totally symmetrical, because they have to accommodate the basement steps.

The walls of the garden are clothed with climbers that tend to merge with the neighbour's adjacent planting, which helps to lose the effect of a long narrow plot confined by walls. It is so often the case in London gardens that the planting in a neighbouring plot is beneficial to your own. It is particularly effective here, as the gardens contrast well against one another.

Although this is essentially a symmetrical garden, elements of asymmetry enliven it – such as the two *Cordyline australis*. There are other anomalies – plants saved from elsewhere or with sentimental attachments (such as a ginkgo, a 30th birthday present). Of the many pots and containers to be found in the garden, some are seasonally planted with white trailing lobelia or marguerites (*Argyranthemum frutescens*), while others contain a pair of standard white wisteria trained over umbrella frames.

The garden really comes into its own at night, especially when it is being used by Margy Fenwick to host a party or for dinner. During these times, atmosphere is created by the use of spot lights both inside and outside the arbour, and by having candles on the long dining table. It is then that the white flowers, and indeed the whole garden, are perhaps at their most effective and magical.

LEFT Pots planted with box topiary are used to articulate the simple paved layout, which has at its centre a circular pool and cast iron fountain. At ground level the garden is much more visually complex.

BELOW Viewed from the pergola-covered dining table at the end of the garden, a new terrace at drawing room level is seen in the background. The dark green of *Ligustrum delavayanum* forms mop-heads of varying size in the beds throughout the garden. This small-leaved privet makes a tighter head than box.

Water and Evergreens

Belgravia

Designers XA TOLLEMACHE WITH GEORGE CARTER

Space and light are at a premium in Belgravia and, when Lord and Lady Astor began to create a new garden, they encountered the typical problems faced by all houses in that grand part of London. Their garden is, in effect, at the bottom of a deep dark well surrounded by tall buildings and walls on all sides. The enclosed feeling is compounded by the magnificent old London plane trees (*Platanus hispanica*) that combine to form a leafy canopy in summer, which filters out almost all the midday sun that might stray in. The garden is also of an irregular shape and any changing of levels was greatly constrained by the mass of tree roots that could not be disturbed by too much excavation or cutting. In the end this last limiting factor more or less determined the levels and the position of the major features.

The brief Lord and Lady Aster gave was to produce an ordered, elegant garden that looks good in the winter and summer and one that can be viewed equally effectively from the basement bedroom as it can from the first floor terrace that leads off the dining room. They also wanted water, preferably a canal, and interesting lighting.

The first problem to solve was how to create an effect of symmetry and order in a totally irregular site that has disparate wall surfaces and two large randomly positioned trees. The trees, like most of their age and stature in London, have Tree Preservation Orders placed on them, so cannot be touched. However, the knobbly boles of their trunks create such bold and interesting features that it would anyway be foolish to try and get rid of them.

The illusion of symmetry was created by axising the canal at an angle to the garden but at right angles to the basement bedroom's French windows. This means that Lord and Lady Astor can sit in bed and look down the canal virtually at eye level. They can also operate the waterworks and lighting from their bed.

The line of the canal determines the geometry of the whole garden, and box hedges in raised brick beds follow its line rather than that of the walls. Large topiary in Versailles

This garden is designed to make
a spectacular *coup d'oeil* from the
house. It is, in effect, at the bottom
of a deep well but the lack of light
has been compensated for by an
increased contrast of light and dark
in the planting and architecture.

cases are arranged symmetrically about this new axis, as are tall Italian cypresses (*Cupressus sempervirens* 'Stricta'); their towering pencil thin shapes make use of the vertical space of the garden and 'read' well from the upper levels.

The central feature of the garden is a lead obelisk with a frostwork surface dripping with water. It is backed by a reflective panel of galvanized steel faced with glass panels, which helps to reflect light into the garden and throws the dark obelisk into contrast. Water emitting from the top falls into the raised pool on which it sits and then runs into the canal. From there, it is pumped back up to the top of the obelisk using a submerged pump. The canal has been lined in black to increase its reflectivity.

Artificial lighting is at a fairly low level so that it will not annoy the neighbours, but it does really bring the watery elements of the garden to life. This is mainly a garden for looking at rather than being in. It has been changed from a dank pit to a lively green space and is the perfect foil to the coolly elegant interior that overlooks it.

ABOVE Tall *Cupressus sempervirens* 'Stricta' have been used at the end of the garden to visually link the upper terrace with the garden below.

PREVIOUS PAGES A raised terrace leading off the dining room looks down on the canal and box parterres below. Strategically placed *Viburnum tinus* standards deliberately block out light from the mews house windows at the end of the garden.

RIGHT A lead obelisk cascades water into a basin. Behind it a screen of galvanized steel covered in glass panels reflects light and provides a background to emphasize its shape.

Georgian meets Jungle

Islington

Designers LESLIE GEDDES-BROWN & HEW STEVENSON

Leslie Geddes-Brown and Hew Stevenson bought their 1800 Islington house fourteen years ago when it had no garden to speak of. Even the classic London brick walls that enclose it to a height of 2m (6ft) fell down shortly after they moved in, so they really did have to start from scratch. Leslie Geddes-Brown has a professional interest in houses and gardens as the well-known journalist and writer on the subject of interiors and gardens. Her husband, a retired newspaper manager, shares her interest in the architectural side of gardening. Like many owners of London gardens they also garden in the country, and it is interesting to compare the similarities and differences in the two approaches to garden design. Their vision of gardening is basically carried through in both, but the differences in scale make for a more concentrated scheme in London with a concern for year-round effect.

Faced with the typical problem of how to deal with a long narrow site, they very sensibly took the view that this is the ideal ground plan for a series of interlinked garden rooms. This gave them the opportunity to create four separate gardens with quite different characters. They like formality, which is a perfect style for using alongside the symmetry of Georgian architecture. However, they also love the sculptural quality of architectural plants and have used them to great effect; these plants provide an essential contrast to the geometry of the rest of the garden.

The sequence of rooms starts with a stone-paved dining terrace right next to the house. This is followed by the second area, which is made of brick paving fronted by a bed of acanthus, clipped euonymous and *Iris foetidus*. All of these architectural plants have year-round foliage. This bed is given structure by the addition of a pair of metal obelisks that I was asked to design specifically for the space. Along with some of the other architectural elements of the garden, including the group of four metal trellis piers and urns next to the house, these help to define the various sections, as well as unify the whole garden.

There are various interlinked
compartments to this Islington
garden. The fountain at the centre
of the sunken circular space is
cunningly contrived from a standard
campagna-shaped urn.

The third section was the most complicated to create. It is a sunken circular garden with a round pool at its centre, into which a *campagna*-shaped urn drips water. This section is insulated from the others by yew hedges, those at the back being punctuated by two staircases that lead to the raised fourth area. This part of the garden has a very attractive symbolic rationale – all the plants in it are chosen for their relationship to classical architecture. So the raised beds above the circular depression are planted with a collection of different acanthus, bay, ivy and daphne. This part of the garden is shaded by a particularly attractive and large evergreen shrub, which is probably a *Cotoneaster* x *watereri* – Leslie Geddes-Brown and Hew Stevenson have had conflicting opinions on the plant's true identitiy. This shrub really is the making of the garden as its open habit means that plants are able to grow below it, but its size and spread can still add a large scale to the overall design, in pleasing contrast to the smaller detail in the subdivisions.

The fourth section provides the background to the whole garden and it is a particularly unexpected element – an

RIGHT The furthest part of the garden, a bamboo jungle planted in gravel, forms the setting for a series of gothick incidents. At the end, a gothick window is framed in dense foliage.

BELOW The small courtyard has been formed out of an L-shaped extension. It has been given architectural definition by four metal trellis piers and urns planted with hops to create a small outdoor dining room.

exotic jungle planted in gravel and made up of a collection of bamboos with the hardy palm *Trachycarpus fortunei*, pittosporum and the odd rambling rose. An *Amelanchier*, seemingly rather out of place in this area, actually really 'reads' as part of the more classical third section, to which it forms an attractive low backdrop. The bamboos tell a story, forming a collection that has sentimental references – this is always a good way to personalize a garden. One of the bamboos comes from a cutting given from the essayist John Ruskin's garden at Brantwood in the Lake District. Another is a rarity from Chile, *Chusquea culeou*, which forms an attractive dense clump on deep olive-green canes. Other of these plants have been chosen for the contrasting scale and texture of their foliage. All of them have a trouble-free hardiness and, most important in this garden, are dog-proof.

This last wilderness area is given the civilizing influence of a charming Regency gothick window, which can just be glimpsed in the wall of the garage that terminates the whole garden. This turns the wilderness into what might be a corner of the Brighton Pavilion – a Georgian view of the exotic quite in keeping with the garden's affinity with the 'Age of Elegance'.

An Oasis of Green

Islington

Designer DIANA YAKELEY

Interior and garden designer Diana Yakeley has designed a garden for herself and her architect husband that is wonderfully controlled and 'furnished', literally as if it were an additional room outside. Unlike many gardens of this kind, plants, rather than hard landscaping, predominate. The planting is rigorously but discreetly clipped and pruned, giving the garden a very architectural quality.

Diana Yakeley started her design with well-defined aims, rather in the way she might approach an interior scheme. She wanted the garden to be an essay in different textures of foliage and shades of green, ranging from lime to bottle and blue/green. The flower colour is limited exclusively to white. On the practical side, the space had to provide an element of privacy both from above and from ground level as well as be a flexible space for seating and dining – rearrangeable according to the time of day. It is, she says, primarily a place to unwind after stressful working days.

The levels of the garden were recast to create a two-tier garden with steps that form an entrance to the larger upper space. Clever use has been made of a concrete soil retention system originally designed for motorways. Axised on the steps is a sort of living temple made up of four clear-stemmed Swedish birches rising from a clipped oblong bed of ivy, chosen because its serrated leaves match those of the birch leaves. Green architecture, which is what this arrangement could be called, is an appropriate way of defining space in London gardens – a greener way of adding structure. The leaf canopy is kept in shape by judicious pruning to give overhead cover without massive height. The perimeter boundaries are obscured by dense planting of climbers – ivies, *Hydrangea petiolaris*, white wisteria and *Schizophragma*.

There is no grass in the garden – often the case in London where shade makes grass thin, grassy areas may be too small to cut easily and heavy wear may turn the grass into a muddy quagmire in winter. Here, the main surfaces have been paved with three subtly different colours; black stable

RIGHT Although this is not a formal garden, it has an ordered geometry that makes every combination of planting, hard surface and furniture into a satisfying abstract composition. Clever juxtapositions of solid and open foliage make the garden into a subtle essay in varied textures of green, only needing the occasional accent of white to make it complete.

BELOW Diana Yakeley has indeed only used white flowers in her elegant green and white outdoor room. Here *Lilium regale* forms one of the many still-life compositions that punctuate the garden.

bricks, black bricks and clay pammetts (square flooring tiles). They are all laid at right angles to the garden perimeters, reinforcing the well-ordered geometry of the site.

When viewing the plan of the garden, it is easy to see that the layout is actually very simple. It is basically made up of two rectangles of paving on different levels, with densely planted beds around the perimeter. Where the levels change, the beds encroach into the middle of the garden, leaving a narrow staircase to link the upper and lower areas. It is the planting that largely articulates the space and makes it an interesting and exciting arrangement of volumes and voids. Successful gardens always have this sculptural concern with the overall organization of space, and it makes no difference how large or small the available space is.

An aspect of this garden that is particularly admirable is the way in which the pots have been arranged. Most of the flowering plants are in containers so that they can be repositioned for maximum effect when they reach their peak of condition. The groupings are as carefully thought out as a still life of objects in an interior would be – the juxtapositions of various flowers and foliage make great sculptural compositions in themselves. At different times of the year there can be found masses of lilies, hydrangea, agapanthus, hostas and helixine. In summer *Lilium regale* and feverfew are in evidence. Later on *Lilium montana*, white agapanthus and *Nerium oleander* 'Alba' take over. In winter, white cyclamens flower while foliage plants such as *Taxus baccata* 'Semperaurea' and *Pittosporum tenuifolium* 'Tom Thumb' work their effect. There are also particularly unusual combinations of plantings, such as Welsh onions alongside flat leaf parsley.

This is a garden designed for year-round effect, using plenty of evergreens to define the layout in winter. Indeed, the large majority of the hundred or so subjects cultivated are evergreen. The skill of the gardener is revealed through this evergreen planting because a sufficient range of colour

The elements that define the main axis are more subtle than in many formal gardens. Two box cones and four clear stems of Swedish birch do the trick and are reinforced by a central box ball and a single steel spiral plant support.

PREVIOUS PAGES Although it is
highly organized, this garden has
a delightfully free-form disposition
of foliage. The concentrated pot
groups, leaving large areas of
paving clear, contribute to the
overall feeling of spaciousness.

LEFT Both *Brugmansia suaveolens*
and *Eucomis bicolor* flower in late
summer. These plants extend the
overall white and green scheme.
Although both are tender, they
will thrive in the walled shelter
of a London garden.

has been found to ensure that it is anything but boring, which massed evergreen can often be. Much use is also made of the stems of deciduous planting, which add a telling graphic element to the winter scene. The garden might be said, though, to be at its peak from June to September, when the white flowering subjects lift the whole effect somewhat. However, the garden can never be described as sombre as there are plenty of bright, sharp colour contrasts whatever the time of year, such as robinia with gleditsia, or the white birch bark seen against dark ivy and black paving.

The neatness, organization and extreme application of refined taste makes Diana Yakeley feel her garden might actually be seen by others as the product of an obsessive and rather buttoned-up personality – like the outdoor equivalent of compulsive dusting! But, on the contrary, to the outsider the garden appears to be a supremely restful haven where nature has been perfected – and surely that is the prime object of gardening?

Surreal

A Sculpture Garden

Gospel Oak

Designer JUDY WISEMAN

This garden is in the tradition of the grand sculpture gardens of Renaissance Italy, albeit scaled down to a North London plot. In particular, it is reminiscent of the weird and symbolic garden of the giants at Bomarzo, near Rome. However, the sculptress who created this garden is very unpretentious about her achievement.

Her sculpture is often formed from casts of body parts, which vary in scale from small parts of limbs right up to life-size figures. These form the subject of the garden and so the planting has been designed as a setting rather than as an end in itself. Bodies and limbs are used with great invention in this garden, cleverly emerging from water or partially hidden by bold foliage. The sculpture, which the artist refers to as 'jewellery for gardens', is used on a life-size scale for particular, bold effects but also crops up in miniature, providing details that really have to be looked for. In the latter category are small metal casts of fists or lips hanging from the branches of trees, like magical fruit from a classical myth. They can also be found sitting on the ground, only partly visible in the grass, like fallen fruit. Judy Wiseman likes the fact that some of these details will inevitably be missed by the casual visitor to the garden – it gives the garden a many-layered richness, and means that there will always be something to be discovered by her guests.

It is the way that the sculpture is integrated into the planting that is so original. The pieces are not classically framed against a clean yew background, but merge with planting such as *Soleirolia soleirolii* (baby's tears), which forms an encasing blanket of green, to fudge the distinction between nature and art. In another part of the garden, a mass of toes and fingers, unrecognizable from a distance, forms a bed edging – a wonderful update of the decorative Victorian edgings that were a ubiquitous part of London gardens in the nineteenth century.

Because the designer is primarily a sculptor she brings an artist's eye to the planting, choosing species that have a three-dimensional quality. She has selected acanthus,

PREVIOUS PAGES Two kneeling figures flank the entrance to one of the garden rooms. This particular area is defined by trained ivy. The garden has been conceived as a kind of outdoor sculpture gallery – the planting insulates works from each other and provides a mysterious framework for their display.

RIGHT A bathing figure partially submerged is constantly cooled by a small waterfall. No figure in the garden is seen in its entirety – they are all only partially glimpsed emerging from foliage, water or paving.

BELOW Casts of fingers and toes emerge from the fissures in paving, with the unnerving implication that a whole body lies below. These are examples of details that aren't immediately seen, making them the more effective when they are noticed.

bamboo, euphorbia and senecio for their bold forms, and because they colonize a site, making it mysterious and jungly. Of course, this sort of planting is not as wild or as uncontrolled as it looks. Great skill has been put into discreet pruning and the provision of contrasting areas, where plain surfaces and clipped foliage make a foil against which the wilderness is thrown into relief.

Judy Wiseman claims she is not good with flowers, and she has a sculptor's mistrust of colour, so this is essentially a garden of contrasting greens, where light and shade create the interest that colour would provide in a flower garden. Grey plantings also add relief here and there, in the form of senecio, lavender and *Artemisia ludoviciana*.

Judy Wiseman constantly adds to the garden and changes the existing plantings – she certainly doesn't see it as a static creation, as the inscription at its entrance reveals: 'A garden is never finish…' This garden has a remarkable air of grandeur for so small a space (15 x 24m/50 x 80ft) and incorporates, without looking cluttered, an enormous range of moods and experiences, as well as pure inventiveness.

LEFT This hanging torso – like a shirt on a washing line with the gruesome addition of hands – is one of the numerous visual jokes in the garden. The jokes are all rather disturbing, in the true spirit of the Surrealists.

BELOW Casts of feet are an update of the Victorian decorative tiles that were used as an edging to borders and paths. These feet are, quite literally, 'pushing up the daisies'.

ABOVE Bronze 'flowers' based on
navels are used throughout the
garden: sometimes on metal stems
as giant lilies, other times in the
water to look like water lilies.

RIGHT A sleeping figure beneath
a blanket of *Soleirolia soleirolii* is
reminiscent of the classical figures
in an eighteenth-century park –
such as the 'Sleeping Nymph' in the
grotto of the gardens at Stourhead
in Wiltshire. It is extraordinary how
many different moods are created in
this garden by the sculpture – each
piece creates its own references
and message.

Colour and Ceramics

Muswell Hill

Designers EARL HYDE AND SUSAN BENNETT

Ceramicist Susan Bennett and film set maker Earl Hyde have been gradually extending their garden by acquiring neighbouring plots and it is now the size of three tennis courts. For them, a garden should have atmosphere, surprises and, most of all, humour. They hate po-faced gardens, and their own is rich in exuberant, colourful fun. This is one of the factors that has made it immensely popular when they open it for the National Garden's Scheme. They get huge pleasure and stimulation from sharing it with the thousand or so visitors they get in the three open days, which are spread across the seasons. The garden is a joint effort but Susan Bennett mainly takes responsibility for the planting, while Earl Hyde develops the architectural side.

The various expansions to the garden have provided welcome inspiration for new developments. The 'Great Wall of China', for instance, was built for a practical reason: to screen a propagating area, which is called by Earl Hyde 'The Forbidden City'. Here, an oriental character was chosen as this gave the opportunity for bright contrasting colours. The bright blue tiles were specially made and fired on site – some of them using the Japanese *raku* method of firing, which gives an interesting crackled lustre to the glaze. The Far Eastern matching blue pots were a lucky local find. Gravel very appropriately covers the surface – this was partly inspired by the fact that a thick layer of ugly tarmac originally covered this area. Set into the circular moon window and the fake door are mirrors designed to dissolve the boundaries.

Another hidden part of the garden has quite a different character. As its centrepiece Earl Hyde has built a circular classical temple, which has been given a surreal twist by being painted in shades of blue with glazed ceramic gold lustre capitals. In its new guise this temple has just received a bell-shaped resin dome with gilded fish-scale tiles. Much fun has been had in this area with the planting: Susan Bennett has parodied a municipal bedding-out scheme in dark and light blue lobelia with cornflowers,

The 'Great Wall of China' was built after the garden was expanded. The bright blue tiles were specially made and fired by the owners. Mirrors set into the windows and doors give the impression of a similar garden beyond.

white marguerites and purple orach. This is seen through a screen of delphiniums and asters.

Planting is designed in this garden to be lively and to reinforce an idea. For example, the Baroque fireplace, which is set against a boundary fence, uses the shrub *Lonicera nitida* 'Baggesen's Gold', to simulate a fiery grate. To create a solid background, the fences are raised with trellis to a height of 2.4m (8ft) and are densely planted with wisteria, various ivies, *Rosa* 'Apple Blossom' and jasmine.

Much use has been made of variegated foliage to lighten the shaded aspects of the garden. Pots are planted up differently every year and Susan Bennett loves luridly coloured foliage plants, such as begonias and coleus.

This is a garden created by two artists. Their studio is at its centre and they love to work outside in their garden whenever they can. In a very real way this surreal garden is a testing ground for their artistic ideas and so it is constantly changing. Every visit to it reveals some fresh, exciting new planting or development.

PREVIOUS PAGES Blue is used to great effect in this garden, both in planting and in structures. The columns of this classical rotunda have been marbled lapis lazuli blue, and the ceramic Corinthian capitals have been fired with a brilliant gold lustre glaze.

RIGHT A stoneware pagoda is lit up for night-time effect, and rises out of one of the garden's three pools. Ceramic faces peer eerily out of the gloom here and there.

BELOW A fireplace has been specially marbled and gives an indoor feel to this outdoor dining area. Golden *Lonicera* has been planted in the grate to suggest fire.

Illusion and Illumination

Muswell Hill

Designer PAUL COOPER

This is the second garden that Paul Cooper has designed for the same client, so both knew the tastes and interests of the other before the project began. An extended family of parents, two children and a grandmother all live in the house, each with their own particular requirements that Cooper had to incorporate into the design. The grandmother wanted a space of her own to grow plants she likes, some of which have particular sentimental associations. The children needed an open play space with a paddling pool. And the parents wanted a better view from the house, the lower floor of which is about 1.2m (4ft) below ground level, as well as a place of escape with a degree of fanciful theatricality. They like jungly plants and their interest in the exotic is reflected inside the house, where leopard skin prints can be found on the upholstery.

Many jungle-like plants have been used in the garden and these are characterized by a boldness of foliage that adds a real lushness to the planting. Many of these plants are not really hardy or suitable for the garden's north facing, dry conditions and have been grown in containers so that they can be taken indoors or supplied with their own special growing conditions. For example, gunnera has been planted in a moisture-retaining pot and bananas and palms survive most of the rigours of winter in pots.

This is a garden full of meaning and symbolism largely reflecting the interests and tastes of the owners. Cooper's cleverest folly is a partly subterranean grotto full of effects. It is circular in plan with stone-faced interior walls and a slate and stone floor. Except for the iron-domed roof that supports climbing plants, it is all below ground level. Set within the walls are a series of back lit 'windows' that contain sheeps' bones displayed on stainless steel rods. These make reference to eighteenth-century grottos that often used animal bones to enrich their structure. Underneath one of the seats is a smoke machine and the chamber is also wired for sound so that they can enjoy a completely theatrical experience that combines light, smoke and music.

This cut-out *trompe l'oeil* vicar is a self-portrait by the garden's designer, Paul Cooper. He presides over the oval lawn, designed at the owner's request to remind him of the South London Oval cricket ground.

The grotto will eventually be embowered with Virginia creeper and passion flower trained over the dome. The surrounding perimeter fences are also planted so that the boundary will soon be concealed by informal planting.

Cooper likes to have a continuing relationship with his clients so that the gardens can evolve over time, responding to new ideas and redefining existing ones. One of the client's obsessions – cricket – has been incorporated in the form of a seated vicar taking tea, while notionally watching a cricket match. He is in reality a self-portrait of Cooper – the fact that he sits overlooking an oval lawn makes reference to the Oval cricket ground, which was close to the client's previous house. A planned future change involves turning the shed into a cricket scoreboard.

In this garden the clients' and designer's views have elided to great effect – they all love symbolism, theatrical effects and breaking planting rules. They believe that a garden is a constantly changing work of art in which the ideas are as important as the plants.

LEFT A sunken grotto next to the house is covered over with climbers that will eventually provide a dense canopy of green. This hidden spot fulfills the traditional function of grottos – to provide a place of retirement and solitude for thought and relaxation.

RIGHT Set into the walls of the grotto, back-lit bones create the sort of *memento mori* that is essential to a place of contemplation. Viewed in the abstract they also make interesting pieces of sculptures.

BELOW The theatrical effects within the grotto include a smoke machine and speakers for sound reproduction. Combined with the subtle lighting, these help to create an amalgam of symbolism, jokes and fun.

Magic in the Grotto

Notting Hill

Designers SARA & CHARLES FENWICK & JANE SEABROOK

This unusually large and well-protected garden in Notting Hill has been given an air of magic and mystery by antique dealer and decorator Sara Fenwick. Her husband Charles, who masterminds the Chelsea Gardener shops and garden centres, and has long been an inspiration to the gardening world, also helped to create the garden. The sheer size of this garden makes it seem like it is in the country rather than in the heart of London. It is full of sculpture and objects but does not look overcrowded; each part of it has an inventive, different character. The areas nearest the house are both sunny and cheerful and have a lush, structural planting of trees and shrubs that shade a terrace.

At the far end of the garden the Fenwicks recently commissioned designer and gardener Jane Seabrook to build an amusing and atmospheric grotto that was inspired by eighteenth-century examples. This dark and shadowy end of the garden has always had a different character to the rest and Sara Fenwick wished to intensify this mood of quiet melancholy with an appropriate building, as well as seating and lighting, to make a visit to this retired and hidden part of the garden an unexpected and slightly surreal experience.

The brief Seabrook was given was to construct a garden within a garden, quite separate and invisible from the rest: somewhere to go on a summer evening to have a quiet, convivial drink or escape from the noise of London. From the house, the area is hidden by a screen of trees and shrubs and the dense shade that this generates has made it an ideal place for a fernery: a rather nineteenth-century idea that accords well with grottos.

Jane Seabrook was the gardening supremo at the Chelsea Gardener, London's most fashionable garden centre, for many years. She has designed the gardens of a host of London's celebrities and socialites. Now retired, she concentrates on the construction of theatrical garden effects. Her first essay in this style was in an earlier garden of Charles Fenwick's, where she created a sublime alpine gorge using antique fragments and a cataract of water.

RIGHT The grotto is surrounded by its own garden, which has quite a different character to the rest of the garden. It also has its own entrance gateway hidden behind a dense shrubbery, which appears by accident when you approach.

BELOW Hidden in the furthest recess of this large Notting Hill garden a new grotto has arisen, making use of a variety of architectural fragments – chunks of tufa, shells and mirrors.

Seabrook designed this new grotto to be built around a framework of cheap breezeblock, which is clad in more expensive materials – tufa, spars and flint – on the outside. The design is loosely based on the poet Alexander Pope's famous grotto at Twickenham. The interior and entrance to the grotto are enlivened with the colour and glitter of broken fragments of mirror, ceramic, shells and spars. Natural light is filtered through a cast iron grille and subtle artificial light makes the interior a magical place to be at night. It is inhabited by partially decayed stone figures that drip with water. These have, in a short space of time, taken on the delightful mossed look of antique sculpture though they are, in reality, fragments of modern reproductions. It is hard to make a grotto look good from the outside as they are essentially interior spaces, but here the varied outline and domed roof have been brilliantly contrived and augmented by flanking 'ruins'. The exterior surface has also been provided with soil pockets so that ferns and mosses can ultimately colonize the walls, to further break up the outline.

ABOVE The main garden is open and sunny. When viewed from the house, there isn't a hint of the hidden recesses to be found, although a lead gardener seems to peer in the direction of the grotto. The contrasts of light and dark, always one of the chief delights of a garden, are skillfully managed in this space.

BELOW A leafy ante room to the grotto
is furnished with a French concrete,
rustic work table and stools. The
planting is purposefully wild and
disordered to create the feeling of
a tangled wood.

OVERLEAF Sara Fenwick's fantastic
grotto chair sets the tone of the grotto
garden with its deliberate air of
neglect. It almost seems to visitors
as if they have stumbled into an
enchanted forest. At night a
glimmering light shines over it
from the grotto's grilled windows.

The grotto garden is entered through a new gateway that demarcates the entrance to this 'other world', which is completely different to the open, sunny quality of the rest of the garden. The furnishing of this part has been carried out with great invention by Sara Fenwick, whose magnificent grotto seat is almost hidden by the jungly undergrowth. This seat is reminiscent of the grotto furniture that was designed by the eighteenth-century architect Thomas Wright – a fitting place to sit for the professional hermits who were sometimes employed by landowners of that era. She is an expert at finding the recherché objects sought out by both decoraters and collectors at her fascinating London shop Myriad Antiques, which has long been a particular place of pilgrimage for the cognoscenti.

Another part of this garden has been furnished with a 1930s set of French rustic stools and a table, all in the shape of barked logs. These are actually made out of concrete although they have patinated to give a pleasantly distressed appearance. All the elements that have been carefully placed in the different areas of this inventive garden combine to create a magical mystical place. In the twilight of a summer evening you can truly imagine that there are fairies at the bottom of this London garden.

Garden Designers

Jonathan Baillie
0589 731141
Jonathan Bell
0207 602 8623
George Carter
01362 668130
Michael Clark and Simon Steele
07931 383773
Ruth Collier
0207 294 9462
Paul Cooper
01544 230 (fax sent
through mobile)
Belinda Eade
(sculptor in stone)
0207 266 0328
David French (architect)
0207 254 7169
Malcolm Hillier
0207 352 9031

Earl Hyde and Susan Bennett
(ceramicists/designers)
0208 883 8540
Charles Jencks
0207 221 1470 (fax)
Christopher Masson
0207 223 6045
Rick Mather
Rick Mather Architects Ltd
0207 284 1727
Michèle Osborne
0208 960 3828
Jason Payne
0208 444 3964
Jane Seabrook
0207 229 5657
Martin Summers
0207 352 9456
Xa Tollemache
01473 890217

John Tordoff
0207 254 5622
Tom Vach (Harper and
Toms Flowers)
0207 792 8510
Matthew Vincent
The Kew Gardener
0208 948 1422
Kim Whatmore
0208 741 2994
Judy Wiseman
(sculptor/designer)
0208 343 2453
Stephen Woodhams
0208 964 9818
Diana Yakeley
Yakeley Associates Design
0207 609 9846

Gardens open to the public under the National Gardens Scheme

Please see the annually published *Gardens of England and Wales* (*The Yellow Book*), published by The National Gardens Scheme, for opening times and details.

Ruth Barclay
St. John's Wood
David French
Hackney
Malcolm Hillier
Chelsea
Earl Hyde and Susan Bennett
Muswell Hill

John Tordoff
Hackney
Judy Wiseman
Gospel Oak
Diana Yakeley
Islington

Index

Acknowledgments

The author and the photographer would like to thank the
owners and designers of the gardens that appear in this book
for allowing us to photograph the sites and to quiz them on how
they came about. They would also like to thank the following
who helped in various ways: Nadine Bazar, Patti Barron,

Jill Billington, Robert and Nicholas Clark, Michael Clark,
Viscount and Viscountess De L'Isle, Denise Glynn,
Jill Hamer, Mr and Mrs Rupert Hambro, Maria Johannsson,
John Powles, Lindsey Price, Elspeth Thompson and
Andrea Whittaker.